Book of Revelation,

Explained

Poem

Bert Hovestadt; William Marrion Branham

(The Whole)
Book of Revelation,
Explained

Poem,

written by Bert Hovestadt

Cover and lay-out: Bert Hovestadt
Front cover picture: New Jerusalem, from aside (see page 11b§19-22)
Back cover picture: New Jerusalem, from above (see page 11b§19-22)

Back cover small picture: Supernatural Cloud photographed over Arizona (USA) in 1963; next it is turned to the right [https://branham.org/en/pictures], the Sign of the Presence of the Son of man (see page 5g§6(8)10)

Publisher: BoD – Books on Demand, Helsinki, Finland
Printing House: BoD – Books on Demand, Norderstedt, Germany

ISBN: 978-952-49-8830-8

Power!

From today may guide my life He,
Who created me,
Who knows all,
knows what is best for me.

From today I have Hope and a Family
on a hopeless earth,
one Big Family,
with God as Father.

In God's Family
you learn love your enemy,
not with own power,
in God's Power.

Lord Jesus thank You,
for washing away my sins!
Lord God thank You,
for Holy Spirit' Power!

Copyright

Peace with God!

^ This explanation of the Book of Revelation of the Bible reveals news of the past, of today, of the near future and of eternity.

In addition, it came forward as a poem.

^ Since September 2020 I had written one page after another for a small group of Finnish believers. Starting from the first chapters of the Book Revelation. And with the final last pages I found that it had divided into three parts, A, B, and C, each 18 pages long, and each A4-page (in the Finnish language with the same font and size) ≤ 60 lines long.

Next I published everything on my new website on the Internet (ilmestyskirja-branham.com/). And soon after, I had translated and published everything in English.

^

^ Constantly improving everything, both versions got their last big change when I had written the Introduction page (0b§Introduction).

Then, 2022-12-13, I found the last main title RECOGNIZE SIGNS OF OUR TIME (page 0c§Preface, along with six other already existing main title pages: 2a§45, 4e§1317, 6m§6(8)10, 8c§89$_1$156, 10a§18 and 12c§1-22).

^ The seven is God's number of perfection and central number in the Book Revelation (seven churches, star messengers, seals, heavenly trumpets and bowls).

God inspired and confirmed all. In this way, He confirmed my copyright to this explanation.

^ He is the God of inspiration, harmony, and beauty.

Just as the world-famous painter Rembrandt had learned to accurately copy God's Creation. He too had drawn many Biblical scenes (~300), for which in the same way ready-made Bible words can be found.

^

^ However, copyright should be considered in a broader sense. The second and more important copyright holder is my Brother in Christ, William Marrion Branham. On every major question, I have relied on his sermons. What is also based on the Bible.

To me he has been Elijah the prophet at the end of the church era. The prophet Malachi had promised his coming in the last verses of the Old Testament {Mal. 4:1-6 (1d§1-3 and 5c§6(8)10 (+5d+5e§6(8)10))}.

^ BBranham had been a Christian minister in the United States (1909-1965). After the Second World War he had started a healing-by-faith movement and a part of his sermons was taped. There had been big meetings, partly all over the world. (Also two in Finland, in the year 1950.)

Over 1,200 of his sermons and sermon series were compiled and published in spoken and transcribed form by the Voice of God Recordings, Jeffersonville, Kentucky, USA. This is 'copyright 2023 by themessage.com' where all rights are reserved.

^

^ In addition, God's Grace I must remember. In 1974, the Lord Jesus had called me, to which I answered 'yes'. Then He had given me the Right/Power to become a child of God (John 1:12).

God's Love had attracted me and actively I began to seek the Kingdom of God and His Righteousness. Then in 1981, God filled me with His Holy Spirit (Mat. 6:33).

^ Two thousand years ago, God had given His Son to be tortured to death by the most terrible death that mankind had invented by then, crucifixion (John 3:16).

Therefore at the name of Jesus every knee should bow and every tongue confess that Jesus Christ is Lord, to the glory of God the Father {Phili. 2:(5-)10-11}.

^ By Jesus' Sacrifice, every human being was redeemed who follows Him in word and deed (Rm. 10:9-11).

This is how I confess: the Lord Jesus Christ would be the chief holder of my copyright.

^

^ According to God's (Book of) Revelation, Christians in the end-time of the churches would be so blind that they would not know to be blind {Rev. 3:17-18 (1a§1-3 and 1c§1-3)}.

However, you don't have to be a believer to understand the apocalyptic events (0c§Preface).

^ Recognize and understand Biblical signs of our time by accepting facts of what can be seen around us.

The Bible is of no private interpretation, It exactly means what it says (2Peter 1:20).

^ In the same way through Jesus Christ can be gotten Peace with God {John (1:1-) 20:19-21}.

By Him you should be saved through faith! Accept and confess that Jesus Christ is your Lord, now! It is absolutely a free Gift of God (Eph. 2:4-8)!

^

Bert Hovestadt
Lahti, Finland

~ ~ ~

0a§Contents

Pages and Titles

0b§Introduction

To everyone who is interested in his/her future

^ The Book of Revelation is the last Book of the Bible, which came directly from God. He had, He has, and He still has much to say (cf. Rev. 1:1, 19).

Two thousand years ago He had spoken, how at the end of the Gentile church ages the church and the world would look like, and what is soon going to happen. Recognize signs of our time!

^ However, knowledge does not save you. Spiritually you only grow when you humble yourself, as Jesus Christ had to humble Himself. We are not more important than Jesus. Find a Bible and read about the Life of Jesus every day, possibly. You do not need to read much, but think about what you have read and possibly pray. God answers people through all kinds of things/people and especially through His Own Channel of Salvation, Jesus Christ. The most important thing in the life of a human being is to accept the Lord Jesus as your personal Saviour and Leader. Then you get the power/right to become a child of God (John 1:12).

^ You must be the small child, what learns (again) to speak with its Heavenly Father. By this attitude, you can be born from above. Study on your knees the Bible, then God will in His Time fulfill you with His Holy Spirit. Then you desire to tell all people the gospel (Acts 2:38, and so on).

God is ready to set you free when you want to be truly free, when you are really sorry for your sins. When you do what you are able to do, God is doing what you are not able to do.

^

^ The explanation is divided in three portions,

A: History of the church, as it had been given in forward:

^ The seven churches in the Book of Revelation have represented seven successive Revival Light ages. They contain outlines and warnings for the believers of the first churches till the believers of our end-time churches.

Already two thousand years ago God knew that before Jesus' Second Coming the believers would not be ready to meet their Lord and Groom. Throughout the time of the Old Testament God had used one great prophet at a time to warn His people. And for our end-time a same kind of prophet had been promised to come.

^ I believe he has been William Marrion Branham. However, everyone has to find that answer in his/her own prayer life. Maybe you find that he is/was Lars Enarson, or Billy Graham, Baruch Korman, David Wilkerson, ..., your pastor, another spiritual leader, ..., a multitude of Elijah prophets, or a future prophet.

But because of the many deceptions in this end-time, approach this subject very carefully!

^

B: The Seven Seals, and God's Own Explanation:

^ Brother Branham did not get the revelations of the Seven Seals just in his study room. He was commanded to move to another town. After that, miraculous things started to happen.

After the revealing of the secrets of the Seven Seals can be believed, that these revelations had come in at least two main ways. One way is, what brother Branham had explained directly.

^ The other way is, what he had said indirectly with the words {from the book: An Exposition of the Seven Church Ages, Introduction (https://table.branham.org/#/en/main + 'Bookmark' + III,IV,V)}: "...., for out of the (Church) Ages come the Seals, and out of the Seals come the Trumpets, and out of the Trumpets come the Vials [Bowls]. [One creates light for the other.]"

In this way every seal belongs to one church age. And with the help of the Seventh and last Seal believers can recognize the spiritual warfare of the end-time and find suitable spiritual weapons.

^

C: Judgments, and the Final Judgment, and Eternity:

^ First, the ready believers are raptured. They are the ones, who during their life have voluntary persevered 'great tribulation, such as has not been' ('Mat. 24:21'; Rev. 7:14; Rev. 20:4).

After that, a period of distress begins, which I have called the Greater tribulation time, 'such as never occurred since there was a nation.' In this way, the difference between those time periods can be seen. The word greater I have used, because it now affects all mankind ('Dan. 12:1').

^ During the Greater Tribulation, the Gospel and Its proclamation returns to 144,000 Israelites. And at the end of it all the Jews of Israel will be freed from their bondages by accepting the Lord Jesus as their personal Saviour.

In the 18th chapter of the Book of Revelation, every Christian has been severely warned throughout the times about a system that would be very beautiful on the outside but very polluted on the inside. Soon it will be destroyed. After this, the Lord Jesus Christ will come and rule the world during the last seventh thousand sabbatical years together with His Bride believers. (According to the Jewish Biblical calendar, about 6000 years have now passed.)

^ After seven thousand years is the Final Judgment. Every person will be judged according to his/her deeds. Next, the City New Jerusalem will come down from Heaven, where God will dwell surrounded by His loved ones.

That's where the earth and every person is going to. To Eternal Happiness or ….

"RECOGNIZE SIGNS OF OUR TIME"

^ In front of you is one explanation of the entire Book of Revelation. This Book came straightly from God and is part of the Bible.

God, Who created the first human being, had not only foreseen the fall of Adam (and Eve and all mankind). He had also planned before the foundation of the earth to come Himself in His Son Jesus as a Lamb. He, our Creator, sacrificed Himself in order to restore His relationship with everyone, whose heart thirsts for God (Rev. 13:8b, 22:17).
^

^ I am Dutch who had moved to Finland with my family in 1996.

In September 2020 in the Finnish language I started this processing of the entire book Revelation together with a few interested Finnish believers. So it has not just been a writing of my thoughts, but a sharing of thoughts and at the same time my inviting to pray for each other. Too, still I thank for correction suggestions and for helping to spread this writing (12a§1-22, address).

^ Mainly I have used the Berean Bible translation for an easy-to-understand entirety. Where necessary I have translated the Bible texts with a word for word translation.
^

^ As the prophet Jonah I've had to warn. The Presence of the Lord Jesus in the air to catch up and meet His Bride believers, would already have been (Easter, April 2022).

This event is also called the rapture or the taking up into Heaven of those believers, who are ready.

^ Jonah warned a big city and God's Judgment would have come. Then its whole population repented, and God had mercy on them (Jonah 3).

Although Jonah's 40 days' prophecy had not been fulfilled, the Lord Jesus referred to him (Mat. 12:39-42).

^ He had preached powerfully. That is why a city of hundreds of thousands of people had turned from their bad ways.

Likewise, the using of the Book Revelation has been an effective tool. A.o. the next pictures can easy be understood:

- In the end-time there is the (anti) Christian bloc of the West and the United States as its leader (4bcd§1317, etc.).
- In the end-time, the world economy will tighten so much that a collapse will inevitably occur (8d§89₁156, etc.).
- In the end-time, all the nations of the world will together attack Jerusalem and Israel (9k§89₁156).
- In the end-time, the world is divided into two, the western countries' and the dictator countries' blocks (9l§89₁156).
- In the end-time, God will allow the fire baptism of the earth what also will resolve the climate crisis (11a§19-22).

^

^ It is possible that the Presence of the Lord Jesus did not yet come and that the judgment period has not yet begun. In the same way as with Jonah. On the other hand, by Easter this entire writing had been completed in Finnish and widely visible on the Internet. It could have been God's explanation and confirmation, because He wants things to be done in faith {Lk. 18:8 (12c§1-22)}.

Later the English translation and website was completed. At another date, which I had mentioned {6m§6(8)10, 12c§19-22}.

^ The Book Revelation helps to understand the Greater tribulation time period after the Rapture. After the church age chapters, the moment of the rapture and this following period show up, although also of events of the past and the future is spoken, Rev. 4-19 {Rev. 4:1 (2a§45)}.

It is the hell on earth, which could turn into the eternal Hell! So seek God now (Isa. 55:6)!

^ In most Bible translations the word presence hasn't been translated with one clear word, as for example with the 'Young's Literal Translation' (https://biblehub.com/1_thessalonians/4-15.htm).

In the Bible 24 times this Greek word parousia occurs (https://biblehub.com/greek/3952.htm).

^ Throughout my writing it is used, 1The. 4:15b, <We who are alive and remain until the presence of the Lord will by no means precede those who have fallen asleep.>

It is an important concept with which for ex. the events in Matthew §24 begin to unfold {Mat. 24:1---14 (6h§6(8)10)}.

^

^ In addition the next general remarks:

- My website with the English (and Finnish) text can be extended only one year at a time (https://ilmestyskirja-branham.com/book-revelation).

So it exists as long as it exists. (You can find the date of a page if it has received an important update in the last thirty days. Changes are underlined where possible and reasonable.)

- At the end has been described a.o. the situation before and after Easter (12c§1-22).

- Many Christians turn to psychiatrists for answers, not to mention yoga, etc. However, God can allow all kinds of problems before He allows complete blindness {Rev. 3:20 (1bc§1-3)}.

God does not change. He does things in His Own Perfect Way. Two thousand years ago the prophet Elijah [John the Baptist] was needed to get the Jews ready. And the coming of a same kind of prophet has been promised to get us Christians (and Jews) ready for the Presence of the Lord Jesus {Mal. 4:1-6 (1d§1-3)}.

This last text was not fulfilled by John the Baptist. In his time he helped to turn only the hearts of the fathers, not the hearts of the children {Lk. 1:17 (1d§1-3)}, Bert

~ ~ ~ ~ ~ ~

1a§1-3

Seven Revivals

Shalom,
^ The book Revelation is a special book. It was the last book of the Bible that came directly from God.
Likewise the first five books of the Bible had come, written down by Moses (cf. Deu. 34:10).
Prayer of them who walk worthy of their calling, bearing with one another in love (Eph. 4:1-2), Bert

¤ The Book Revelation is the Revelation of Jesus Christ given to Him by God. From God came the prophetic thoughts, what first the churches would need, and in the future the people of Israel. It was given by Jesus Christ to His angel. And after that the apostle John received it (Rev. 1:1).
A miraculous revelation of which John, the only still living disciple of the Lord Jesus, wanted to testify as regards everything he had seen, that it was the word of God and the testimony of Jesus Christ (Lk. 6:13; Rev. 1:2).
¤ Christ is the Head and Lover of the Church (Eph. 5:23-27).
He is God's Plan of Salvation for all mankind (Acts 4:12).
¤ Our only Hope is the Coming of Jesus/God (Rev. 1:7-8), Rev. 1:7a, < Behold, he is coming with the clouds,>
For this the book Revelation prepares, and this is what Jesus says at the end, Rev. 22:20, <"Yes, I am coming soon.">
¤
¤ If you keep the Book Revelation, you will be blessed and Heaven will open to you (cf. Rm. 4:6-8), Rev. 1:3, <Blessed is the one who reads, and they that hear the words of the prophecy, and obey what is written in it; because the time is near.>
Jesus Christ is the Word of God, Which became Flesh and by Which Life and Light came (John 1:1-5 and 9-14).
¤ God did in Jesus what God had demanded in His Word. God let Himself in Jesus be crucified. In this way God's prophetic Word had spoken and is speaking, Rev. 19:10b, <The testimony of Jesus is the spirit of prophecy.>
Woe to them who add something to it or take something away (Rm. 3:4; Rev. 22:18-19).
¤

¤ The Prophetic Word has enormous power from God's point of view. Two thousand years ago, much had been foretold about the life of Jesus Christ. And among the Jewish people, Jesus fulfilled all those prophecies (Lk. 24:44).

In the same way, He bluntly declared to his fellow citizens that no prophet has been honored in his hometown without much more explanation (Lk. 4:16-30 and especially verse 24).

¤ And so on. To His cousin John the Baptist, when in prison he could not (anymore) believe everything, He answered (Lk. 7:1-23), Lk. 7:22b-23, <"Go back and report to John what you have seen and heard: The blind receive sight, the lame walk, the lepers are cleansed, and the deaf hear, the dead are raised, the good news is preached to the poor, 23. and blessed is the one who does not fall away on account of Me.">

This was based on several texts of the prophet Isaiah as regards the coming Messiah, for example, Isa. 61:1-2a (Lk. 4:18-19), <The Spirit of the Lord GOD is on Me, because the LORD has anointed Me to preach good news to the poor. He has sent Me to bind up the brokenhearted, to proclaim liberty to the captives and freedom to the prisoners, 2. to proclaim the year of the LORD's favor, ...>

¤

¤ Imprisoned for his faith, the apostle John had been expelled to the prison island of Patmos. It was the year 96 AD. He was seeking the Presence of God, he was 'on the Lord's day in the Spirit' (Rev. 1:10a).

Suddenly the Lord Jesus stood behind him. When he saw Him, he fell at His feet like a dead man. But the Lord Jesus reassured him and told him something miraculous (Rev. 1:10b-20), Rev. 1:20, <".... The mystery of the seven stars you saw in My right hand and of the seven golden lampstands {is this}: The seven stars are the messengers/angels of the seven churches, and the seven lampstands are the seven churches.">

¤ He got among others seven letters from the Lord Jesus for the churches in seven Asian cities. The nearest large port city on the mainland was Ephesus. After that came the other cities in the same order as in the book Revelation, Smyrna, Pergamum, Thyatira, Sardis, Philadelphia and Laodicea (Rev. 1:4-11).

But these events of Light would be more than just letters to seven churches, (Rev. 2-3).

¤ The stars together with the lampstands would be seven huge Lights, seven events of Light, just as Jesus Christ Himself had come as the Light (John 1:4-5).

Seven consecutive ages, such as the Feast of Unleavened Bread (the Lord's Supper / Communion) was celebrated for seven consecutive days. At the beginning the Passover lamb had been sacrificed, and after the Sabbath, on Sunday, a Sheaf of the Firstfruits had been raised to God. All three Feasts Christ had fulfilled (Lev. 23:4-14; Lk. 22:1-20).

¤ Seven successive Light periods, Revival events, Revival ages. For many churches at the same time (Rev. 2:7; 2:11; etc.).

Next, these seven (spiritual) Revivals with their messengers/angels will be further discussed.

Seven Ages and Messengers

Shalom,
^ Relatively quickly I deal with the church ages. Much deeper and wider it can be done, what I will do in part later. But in the beginning the getting of an overview of the book Revelation is more important.
^ Thanks for any correction, comments, encouragement, prayers, etc.
With the prayer of believers who carry another's burdens (Gal. 6:2), Bert

¤ In 70 AD Rome had destroyed Jerusalem (and its apostolic center) and among others the apostle John and the mother of Jesus, Mary, had settled in the city of Ephesus (cf. John 19:27).
In 96 John was Jesus' last living disciple/apostle. Times were hard and there was much persecution. Possibly John was boiled for 24 hours in oil before he was deported as a witch to the prison island of Patmos. Though, his presence near the church in Ephesus confirmed that it was the spiritual center of the churches of that time (Rev. 2:1-7), Rev. 2:7a, <".... He who has an ear, let him hear what the Spirit says to the churches. ....">
¤ To seven churches the Lord Jesus had written His heartfelt messages. In the beginning He had referred to some of His Attributes (Rev. 2:1, 8, 12, etc.).
For the church of John in Ephesus it had been an emergency message. Its lampstand would be soon removed out of its place, if it did not repent (Rev. 2:4-5), Rev. 2:4, < But I have this against you: You have abandoned your first love.>
¤ From John the first runner left for the first stop. He had among others the task of conveying the personal message of Jesus Christ to the messenger of the church, Rev. 2:1, etc., <To the messenger/angel of the church in Ephesus write: '.... ....'>
The messenger/angel in question (the Greek word 'angelo' ['angel']) was a believer on earth, as the basic meaning of that word is messenger. Only in special situations, when it relates to heavenly beings, the translation would be angel. Throughout the Book of Revelation this should be remembered.
¤ Already was explained, that the church in every town represented one Revival period for many churches. A total of seven Revival periods had been announced. It was the mystery of the lampstand (1a§1-3).
In addition, the messengers of the churches would represent seven different star apostles. It was the mystery of the stars (1a§1-3, =), Rev. 1:20, <.... The seven stars (in My right hand) are the messengers/angels of the seven churches. ....>
¤ The undisputed star messenger of the Ephesian church age had been the apostle Paul. He had been absolutely true to the Word, done the work in the Power of the Holy Spirit and he had the evident fruit of his God given ministry, multitudes of Gentiles had come to faith. More than half of the letters of the New Testament he had written. Even,

he had been the first apostle of the revival of the church in Ephesus, thus this Revival had begun, about 53 A.D. (Acts 19).

With sound teachings and his self-sacrificing way of life he had equipped the churches. His first love for God was never extinguished.

¤

¤ When the revivals of the Ephesian church age everywhere had extinguished, Jesus had removed its lampstand. But active believers, hungry and thirsty, had previously begun to pray to the Lord God for a new revival. When the believers of the Smyrna age had been ready for it, the next Revival had begun, and at some point the next star messenger appeared.

Of the seven ages, only in two the believers would act so well, or the circumstances would be so harsh, that to them were to be given only words of encouragement, Smyrna and Philadelphia.

¤

¤ In revival circles has somehow been accepted that, after the (Dark) Middle Ages, the Reformation of 1517 on the European continent represents the revival period for the fifth church, the Sardis' church (Rev. 3:1-6).

Under Luther's leadership the truth had been rediscovered that only through faith man can become righteousness, Rm. 1:17, <For the gospel reveals the righteousness of God that comes by faith from start to finish, just as it is written: "The righteous will live by faith.">

¤ Regrettably this Revival did not go farther on. A new Revival was needed (Rev. 3:7-13).

During the Philadelphian church age the blessing of a holy life was widely found back in Britain, with the birth of the Methodist Movement (later Church), the Salvation Army, and many mission societies. Next in the United States it spread on a large scale (cf. Hep. 12:10b-14).

¤ Also this Revival died out little by little. A last Revival was needed, the Laodicean church age Revival, the Azusa Street revival, the worldwide Revival of the Pentecostal churches. It began in 1906 in the city of Los Angeles. Then was found that the gifts of the Holy Spirit would be part of the life of every believer (Rev. 3:14-22).

But the message to the Laodicean church tells, that this Revival changed. For later the Lord Jesus is only found from the outside of this church (Rev. 3:20)....

State of the End-Time Church

Shalom,
^ This time a part of my testimony.
Prayer, even in our weaknesses (2Cor. 12:10), Bert

¤ Last time I wrote about the church in Laodicea and its significance for us end-time believers. For decades, this had been a familiar explanation to me. But in the spring of 2012, I noticed that my spiritual state had become similar.
The spiritual fruits of my life were too little or too small. Something didn't work. I was even depressed.
¤ I was a similar spiritual child, what had been predicted. Also I had given a too good picture of myself, Rev. 3:17a, <You say, 'I am rich; I have grown wealthy and need nothing.' ....>
There had come across what I had been trying to avoid. My facade didn't work. I did not (longer) feel that the Lord God was with me.
¤ A year earlier, I had felt guided by the Holy Spirit to join a church. Before that in Finland, I had not been a member of any church. However, everywhere we need each other, especially when the day of Jesus' Coming is very near (Heb. 10:25, 37).
The best way to help myself was to learn to participate. My best act of repentance was to accept that I am as bad or good a believer, as this church and other end-time churches look like in the eyes of God.
¤ But e.g. the following things the Holy Spirit demanded of me. I had to begin to testify with cold or hot words and deeds. To neighbors and so on (cf. Rev. 3:15).
In addition, It instructed me to tell believers that the Second Coming / Presence of the Lord Jesus in the clouds will take place within a year. Then the believers who are ready, are raptured into Heaven, Mat. 24:36-44.
¤ As the prophet Jonah I have had to preach the sermon of God {Jonah 3:1-4 (also 0c§Preface)}.
Thus I have become ready to act and write on God's terms all, what you read here.
¤
¤ In the end-time, Jesus Christ stands before the door of the church in Laodicea, Rev. 3:20, <".... Behold, I stand at the door and knock. If anyone hears My voice and opens the door, I will come in and dine with him, and he with Me. ....">
He, the written and living Word of God, is no longer accepted as such in the churches of this end-time (cf. John 1:1-3, 14).
¤ Although the gifts of the Holy Spirit had been rediscovered (1b§1-3, Rev. 3:14-22).
But if the Giver of the gifts is not served as the first one, whatever kind of heavenly gifts is not relevant.
¤
¤ Where is Christ when He is no longer in the church? But the revival would not have gone out, because He is still visible. Only the revival would have moved to somewhere else.

Confirmation for this claim is, that also from Laodicea believers are raptured to Heaven, Rev. 3:21-22, <"…. To the one who overcomes, I will grant the right to sit with Me on My throne, just as I overcame and sat down with My Father on His throne. 22. He who has an ear, let him hear what the Spirit says to the churches.">

¤ Every believer is exhorted to act, Rev. 3:18-19, <"…. I counsel you to buy from Me gold refined by fire so that you may become rich, white garments so that you may be clothed and your shameful nakedness not exposed, and salve to anoint your eyes so that you may see. 19. Those I love, I rebuke and discipline. Therefore be earnest and repent. ….">

You are worth gold, when you are in the Body of the Lord Jesus in harmony with your position. When you are in God's Clock the little movement, what is needed there. Then the world sees, what the right time is (cf. 1Cor. 12).

¤ White robes are your righteous acts (Rev. 19:8).

Passport, ticket, instructions, etc. must be picked up at the correct locations. Eye-salve is needed to know these places.

¤ We must always be ready to leave for the land of Israel, which is the Land of God (Lev. 25:23), and whose future Capital Jerusalem awaits in Heaven {cf. Gal 4:26 (11b§19-22)}. Even today, in the blink of an eye, that Moment of Departure may come {1Cor. 15:(50-)51-52(-53) (2a§45 and 5d§6(8)10)}!

¤

¤ In the Gospel according to Matthew the Lord Jesus got three questions about the future, and before He answered He gave words of warning {Mat. 24:1-3, and 4-14 (6h§6(8)10)}.

Firstly, He gave details of the moment of the destruction of the temple {Mat. 24:15-21 (3e§12)}.

¤ Secondly, He spoke about the sign of His secret Coming/Presence. When the Rapture will take place it is like a lightning message to the loved ones and to the closest friends of the raptured believers who are left all over the world (Mat. 24:40b ja 41b), Mat. 24:(21-)27-28, <…. 27. For just as the lightning comes from the east and flashes as far as the west, so will be the coming/presence of the Son of Man. 28. Wherever there is a carcass, there the eagles/vultures will gather.>

Eagle believers fly higher. They see already now Christ outside of the churches (Rev. 3:20).

John the Baptist of the End-Time

Shalom,
^ The word for angel in the New Testament I discussed already (1b§1-3, Rev. 2:1).
Miraculously, in the Hebrew Old Testament, a similar word 'malak' is used, which has almost two identical meanings, messenger and angel, and also its literal basic meaning is messenger. Even crosswise, their connectedness is visible. In both places there is talked of John the Baptist, Mal. 3:1a, <"Behold, I will send My messenger (/my angel), who will prepare the way before Me. ....">
^ And in the New Testament, Mat. 11:10, <".... This is the one about whom it is written: 'Behold, I will send My messenger (/my angel) ahead of You, who will prepare Your way before You.' ....">
Prayer of them who discipline their own bodies (1 Cor. 9:27), Bert

¤ Already two thousand years ago, God knew that before the Second Coming of Jesus, believers would not be ready. He had known the same before the First Coming of Jesus. His own people of the kingdom tribe Judah had not been ready. That is why John the Baptist had to come.

In his time John the Baptist had gotten the people of Jerusalem and of the countryside of Judea on the move. It had been a special and big revival just before Jesus Christ began His Life Mission. Every Jew had begun to feel a sting in his heart. Even the spiritual leaders of the country, although he had criticized them sharply (e.g., Mat. 3:1-12).

¤ His task had been to turn the hearts of the fathers and forefathers of the Jewish people to the children, that is, to Jesus and His first apostles. What the angel had said to his father Zechariah, Lk. 1:17, <".... And he will go on before the Lord in the spirit and power of Elijah, to turn the hearts of the fathers to their children and the disobedient to the wisdom of the righteous—to make ready a people prepared for the Lord.">

What was God's best solution then is still His best solution. God does not change. As He had in Old Testament's times almost always used one great prophet, alone (cf. Eccl. 3:14-15).

¤

¤ The mission of the Elijah of our day is found in the last verses of the Old Testament. It is the same turning of the hearts of the fathers and forefathers of the Jewish people. But beyond that, he must turn the hearts of the believers of the Gentiles to Jesus and His apostles, according to Mal. 4:1-6, <"For behold, the day is coming, burning like a furnace, ..." says the LORD of Hosts. .... 4. "Remember the law of My servant Moses, the statutes and ordinances I commanded him for all Israel at Horeb. 5. Behold, I will

send you Elijah the prophet before the coming of the great and awesome Day of the LORD. 6. And he will turn the hearts of the fathers to their children, and the hearts of the children to their fathers. Otherwise, I will come and strike the land with a curse.">
After the ages of the churches, the time period of the Greater tribulation begins, at the end of which the whole earth will burn like an oven. The prophet Malachi had in his time spoken to the Jewish people. Among other things, that's why is talked about the Law of Moses. Then with John the Baptist the Old Testament and its Law closed. Now the chosen ones of the Gentile nations and the Jewish people must prepare to meet their Lord in the upper air. When these elect are taken up, the New Testament closes and the proclamation of the Gospel and the teaching of the Law will return to the Jewish people.

¤

¤ Many revival movements say that there are still big revivals in the Third World. Thus, apostasy in the former Christian Western world would not yet be fulfilling the signs of apostasy, as it must happen before the Presence of the Lord Jesus on the clouds. Therefore, it would not yet be the right time for all the changes, among others the appearing of the Antichrist (the child of perdition), 2The. 2:3b-4aa, <For (that day shall not come) until the apostasy have first come, and the man of lawlessness, the child of perdition, have been revealed, 4aa. that adversary,>

Anyway, those revivals aren't that big. In Korea, for example, there would have been a huge revival throughout the 20th century. Yet today in South Korea, all Christians together make up less than a third of the population. Growth has almost come to a halt and young people have begun to leave the church. And North Korea is the worst dictatorship in the world. For Christians with their family members it means genocide.

¤ In Europe, all Christians were a total of almost 100% of the population. Now only a couple of percent believes in the Lord Jesus and reads the Bible regularly. Also here the evolution theory was invented, which turned the elite worldwide away from the Christian culture {cf. Darwin (9j§89₁156)}.

We live very close to the rapture, the taking up of believers before the horrors of the Greater tribulation time. And again, we may wonder why the Elijah of our time did not come? As Peter, James and John suddenly noticed. Jesus was soon to die, but Elijah was in heaven. That is why they asked Jesus (Mat. 16:21-17:13), Mat. 17:10b, <"Why then do the scribes say that Elijah must come first?">

¤ And that wouldn't be our only question.

Where Jesus Christ of our day can be found? That important question had raised up the last time (Rev. 3:20a).

¤ Peace has been promised to us (cf. Rev. 3:20b).

However, it will not come without our zealousness and our approving of God's Discipline (Rev. 3:19).

~ ~ ~

2a§45

"HEAVEN"

Shalom,
^ Seeking and doing God's Will would be the most important thing anyone can do in their life (cf. Mat. 7:21).
Prayer of them who want to be a beautiful garland/crown in the hand of the LORD, Bert

¤ The fourth and fifth chapters of Revelation would be more than aha topics. Heaven is opened for us!
The place where God is!! Where He sits on His Throne (Rev. 4:2-3)!!!
¤ At one time Jesus Christ had answered Peter about John, John 21:23, <"If I want him to remain until I return, what is that to you?">
In this way was shown to John, as the only still-alive apostle of Jesus, what was to happen in the ages of the churches (Rev. 1-3), and the time after that, Rev. 4:1, <After this I looked and saw a door standing open in heaven. And the sound/voice I had previously heard speak to me like a trumpet was saying, "Come up here, and I will show you what must happen after these things.">
¤ The voice was still the trumpet voice of Jesus Christ (Rev. 1:10).
When the ages of the churches are completely over and the last trumpet sounds, the believers will be taken up into Heaven, as happened to the apostle John (cf. 1Cor. 15:50-53; 1The. 4:14-5:2).
¤
¤ A rainbow is seen around God's Throne (Rev. 4:3b).
It is the sign of the Covenant of Jesus {cf. Gen. 9:8-17; Mal. 3:1b (also 2b§45)}.
¤ In the vicinity of the throne of God are raised 24 respectable believers who have received thrones, Rev. 4:4, <Surrounding the throne were twenty-four other thrones, and on these thrones sat twenty-four elders dressed in white, with golden garlands/crowns on their heads.>
These are not angels. Angels have no crowns, and no thrones. They are people who were bought with the Blood of Jesus Christ (Rev. 5:8-10).
¤ They had been bought like slaves. But still, each of them had a garland/crown!
Likewise, if we win, we will receive for example the garland/crown of life (!), Rev. 2:10b-11, <"'…. Be faithful even unto death, and I will give you the garland/crown of life. 11. He who has an ear, let him hear what the Spirit says to the churches. The one who overcomes will not be harmed by the second death.>

These elders had well embraced in their lives, where they had come from and where they had received their victory power, Rev. 4:10-11, <the twenty-four elders fall down before the One seated on the throne, and they worship Him who lives forever and ever. They cast their garlands/crowns before the throne, saying: 11. "Worthy are You, our Lord and God, to receive glory and honor and power, for You created all things; by Your will they exist and came to be.">

¤ When in this life you become a beautiful crown in the hand of the LORD, one will be gotten in the future (cf. Isa. 62:3).

The apostle Paul called the people who had been given to him to lead to Jesus, his garlands/crowns (Phili. 4:1).

¤ Thrones also have jurisdiction, as it is seen in the millennial kingdom (Rev. 20:4).

And at the end, every man must stand before the Throne of God's Judgment (Rev. 20:11-15).

¤ When John wrote everything, there was still the age of Grace. But in the picture of the fourth chapter, lightnings, sounds/voices, and thunders came from the Throne of God (Rev. 4:5a).

It tells of the temporary Final Judgment of God at the end of the Seventh and Last Trumpet period {Rev. 11:15-19 (also 8e§89₁156)}, Rev. 11:19, <Then the temple of God in heaven was opened, and the ark of His covenant appeared in His temple. And there were lightnings, and sounds/voices, and thunders, and an earthquake, and a great hail(storm).>

¤

¤ Of the twenty-four elders twelve are apostle representatives of the pagan churches, Mat. 19:28, <Jesus said to them, "Truly I tell you, in the renewal of all things, when the Son of Man sits on His glorious throne, you who have followed Me will also sit on twelve thrones, judging the twelve tribes of Israel. ….">

And twelve represent the people of Israel. From the beginning they have been a people of twelve tribes (Gen. 37:9-10).

¤ In the end they all will be found of the Jerusalem of the New Heaven and the New Earth, Rev. 21:12-14, <The city had a great and high wall with twelve gates inscribed with the names of the twelve tribes of Israel, and twelve angels at the gates. 13. There were three gates on the east, three on the north, three on the south, and three on the west. 14. The wall of the city had twelve foundations bearing the names of the twelve apostles of the Lamb.>

God bless you, pilgrim, Rev. 21:7, <The one who overcomes will inherit all things, and I will be his God, and he will be My son.>

Seven Spirits of God

Shalom,
^ Prayer of them who, together with the Holy Spirit, wish to say to everyone, Rev. 22:17, < "Come!" Let the one who hears say, "Come!" And let the one who is thirsty come, and the one who desires the water of life drink freely.>
Receiving the Gift of the Holy Ghost would be the most important event of our life (Acts 2:38), Bert

¤ There is one Holy Spirit. But in Heaven is seen that It appears in 7 different ways (cf. 1Cor. 12:8-11), Rev. 4:5b, <Before the throne burned seven torches of fire. These are the seven Spirits of God.>

Similarly it was written at the beginning of the book Revelation, Rev. 1:4-6, <John, To the seven churches in the province of Asia: Grace and peace to you from Him who is and was and is to come, and from the seven Spirits before His throne, 5. and from Jesus Christ, …. 6. …. .>

¤ This greeting can be compared to the initial greetings of Paul's epistles, as in 1Cor. 1:3, <Grace and peace to you from God our Father and the Lord Jesus Christ!>

Paul greeted alone from the Heavenly Father and the Lord Jesus, as they were both in Heaven.

¤ But he did not greet from the Holy Spirit, because It was here on the earth. This is one possible explanation. Before, here the Holy Spirit had fully filled Jesus (Lk. 3:21-4:1).

And when Jesus was carried up into Heaven, the Holy Spirit returned in the believers during the Feast of Pentecost (Acts 1-2).

¤ When of Jesus was spoken as the Lamb of God, is found (Jn. 1:29, 36), Rev. 5:6, <…. a Lamb who appeared to have been slain, …. The Lamb had seven horns and seven eyes, which represent the seven Spirits of God sent out into all the earth.>

A horn represents power, just as the Holy Spirit is the Power (e.g. Lk. 24:49).

¤ In addition, to the seven different Powers belong seven Eyes.

The Seven Spirits were sent into all the world, like the Lord Jesus sent the Holy Ghost (cf. Jn. 14:16-26; 15:26).

¤ It is thus seen that in John's greeting these 7 Spirits and the Holy Spirit are one and the same thing. And Jesus Christ is Jesus Christ. Would then 'who is and who was and who is to come', be the 'Heavenly Father'? Usually such announcements are found of Jesus (for example Heb. 13:8).

However, Jesus Christ is the same God, Jn. 14:11, <"…. I am in the Father and the Father is in Me …."">

¤ In this way, the Heavenly Father has all the qualities that Jesus has. The Father in Heaven is even greater than Jesus, when He was here on earth (Jn. 14:28).

Thus He who is and who was and who is to come would be here the Heavenly Father (Rev. 21:22).
¤

¤ Outside of the book Revelation, the same seven Spirits can only be found in the book of Zechariah. Jesus Christ is the Root Sprout of David (Rev. 5:5), Zec. 3:8-9, <"…. Hear now, O high priest Joshua, you and your companions seated before you _indeed they are men who are a sign {of what is to come}._ For behold, I am going to bring My servant, sprout. 9. See the stone I have set before Joshua; on that one stone are seven eyes. Behold, I will engrave on it an inscription, declares the LORD of Hosts, and I will remove the iniquity of this land in a single day. ….>

The LORD of hosts, the LORD Sebaot, announced to the leaders of Judah the coming of the Sprout. There the seven Eyes were involved, all the Spirits of God, the Holy Spirit in manifold Power. They were men of the prophetic sign because they had begun to rebuild their temple of God after the exile of Babylon. The temple was needed because Jesus Christ was coming to it (Mal. 3:1b; Heb. 13:20), the Lord, the Messenger (/Angel) of the Covenant.

¤ In connection with the same event Zechariah was told the word of the LORD to Zerubbabel, one of the leaders, Zec. 4:6, <"…. Not by might nor by power, but by My Spirit, ….">

Here, too, it is seen that one Spirit in the singular, and the seven Spirits of God and the seven Eyes of Jesus would be one and the same thing, Zec. 4:10, <"…. But these seven eyes of the LORD, which scan the whole earth, ….">
¤

¤ In the first chapter of Revelation, the Lord Jesus stood in the middle of the lampstands with the stars in his hand. It is dark. The lamps would give light, the Light of the Oil of the Holy Spirit. And the stars would shine and reflect the Light of the Sun, the Light of God, the Living Word of God (Rev. 1:12-20).

First, Jesus Christ was the Light of God two thousand years ago. And since then, the Holy Spirit has given Light through the church in this by sin cursed world. The church at Ephesus represented the first revival period. But when the first love of the believers of that time disappeared, its lampstand was removed from its place (1b§1-3, Rev. 2:5).

¤ Everything had been in the revival of Ephesus. The Power and Gifts and Guidance of the Holy Ghost. The Spoken and Living Word of God. On the lamp base of the Menorah, all 7 lamps burned.

Next, figuratively speaking, God drew one part of his Spirit back to Heaven. Thus, the next revival was not that bright.

Lamb of God

Shalom,
^ As Christians, we are called to become children of God, and together with Christ heirs (Rm. 8:17).
Prayer of them who wish to worship God in Spirit and in Truth (John 4:24), Bert

¤ The most exciting moments of mankind are described in the fifth chapter of Revelation. For good reason the apostle John wept very much. There was no one in heaven, or on earth, or under the earth, worthy to open the book scroll in God's hands, which was sealed with seven seals (Rev. 5:1-4).
John knew, like everyone else there, that this scroll was vital to him and his spiritual brothers and sister. All creation would have been lost! But something had been kept secret, as one of the elders told him, Rev. 5:5, <"Do not weep! Behold, the Lion of the tribe of Judah, the Root of David, has triumphed to open the scroll and its seven seals.">
¤ And suddenly, amid the throne and the four beasts, and amid the elders, stood a Lamb as if it had been slain; it had seven horns and seven eyes (Rev. 5:6a).
When Jesus Christ had come to be baptized by John the Baptist, he had witnessed and cried out (John 1:15-37), John 1:29b, <"Look, the Lamb of God, who takes away the sin of the world! ....">
¤ He had sat on the throne of God at the right hand of the Power (e.g. Mat. 26:64).
And when He came and took the Scroll, the ones present threw themselves before the Lamb and sang a new song about the very foundations of life of the humans in Heaven (Rev. 5:7-9), Rev. 5:9b, <"And by Your blood You purchased for God those from every tribe and tongue and people and nation. ...."
¤
¤ After Adam (and Eve) had sinned, the right to live forever was denied to them (Gen. 3:22).
At the same time the trespass of this man (and woman) had brought condemnation for all men. But two thousand years ago the many were made righteous through the obedience of another one man (Rm. 5:15-19)!
¤ During His ministry, Jesus Christ had said that unless you eat the Flesh and drink the Blood of the Son of Man, you have no life within yourself. Therefore, many of his disciples had left (John 6:53, 66).
But the last time He celebrated the Passover Communion with His disciples who followed Him to the end, He explained, Lk. 22:19-20, <"This [broken bread] is My body, given for you; do this in remembrance of Me." 20. In the same way, after supper He took the cup, saying, "This cup is the new covenant in My blood, which is poured out for you. ...."
¤

¤ The gospel speaks of Him, Who was led like a sheep to the slaughter (cf. Acts 8:26-39).

He is, 'Jesus Christ, the faithful Witness/Martyr',[a] Rev. 1:5-6, <the firstborn of the dead,[b] and the ruler of the kings of the earth.[c] To Him who loves us and has released us from our sins by His blood,[d] 6. who has made us to be a kingdom, priests to His God and Father—to Him be the glory and power forever and ever! Amen.[e]>

a) Jesus Christ had been ready to give up His Equality with God, to become like men, and to be obedient to His Father in all things, until the death of the cross (Phili. 2:5-11; Rev. 5:11-14).

b) Jesus Christ and God are the same God who created all things (Rev. 4:11), Col. 1:15-18, <The Son is the image of the invisible God, the firstborn over all creation. 16. For in Him all things were created, things in heaven and on earth, visible and invisible, whether thrones or dominions or rulers or authorities. All things were created through Him and for Him. 17. He is before all things, and in Him all things hold together. 18. And He is the head of the body, the church; He is the beginning and firstborn from among the dead, so that in all things He may have preeminence.>

c) He is the King of kings and the Lord of lords, who at the beginning of the millennial kingdom will first shatter the reign of all nations, before He shepherds them with an iron scepter (Dan. 2:44-45; Rev. 12:5; 19:11-16), 1Cor. 15:22-24, <For as in Adam all die, so in Christ all will be made alive. 23. But each in his own turn: Christ the firstfruit; then at His presence, those who belong to Him. 24. Then the end will come, when He hands over the kingdom to God the Father after He has destroyed all dominion, authority, and power.>

d) The creation waits in eager expectation for the revelation of those who are led by God's Spirit (Rm. 8:4, 8:9-19), 1Pet. 2:20b-21, <But if you suffer for doing good and you endure it, this is commendable before God. 21. For to this you were called, because Christ also suffered for you, leaving you an example, that you should follow in His footsteps:>

e) After the first resurrection, they/we will reign in the next millennial kingdom, and after this (Rev. 20:4-6), Revelation 22:5b, <and they will reign forever and ever.>

~ ~ ~

A3 (Revelation §12, Spiritual War)

3a§12

Two Signs in Heaven

Shalom,
^ §12 is the most central part of the Book Revelation. Likewise, God's most central and deep plans are found.
Prayer of them who firm in faith resist the Devil, Bert.

¤ Chapter 12 speaks of two signs, the first of which is great. It is a woman clothed in the sun, and the moon under her feet, and a crown of twelve stars on her head (Rev. 12:1).
The same features are found only once in the Bible. When it comes to Jacob/Israel, his wife and his twelve sons (Gen. 37:9-10).
¤ The sons of Israel are the ancestors of the Jewish people. And later this woman gave birth to the Lord Jesus (Rev. 12:2, 5).
God's chosen people represented (and will represent) this Woman, seen in Heaven (Deu. 7:6-8).
¤ In reality it is a copy or shadow of Her (cf. Heb. 8:5).
New Jerusalem She is called. She represents God's Freedom Covenant and Family (Gal. 4:24 and 26).
¤ It is the Covenant of the Blood of Jesus, where God's Law is put into the hearts of believers (Heb. 10:16).
It is the Body of the Lord Jesus, Gods' Family, into which one is baptized by the Holy Spirit (1Cor. 12:13).
¤
¤ The second sign in Heaven is a huge fire-red dragon with seven heads, ten horns, and seven royal crowns on its heads (Rev. 12:3).
When Jesus was born, the Roman state represented this dragon, as it was the sixth head of the dragon. Or better said, it was a copy or shadow of the sixth head {Rev. 17:10a (4a§1317)}.
¤ For example, king Herod, as part of this state, sought to kill Him in Bethlehem (Mat. 2:16; Rev. 12:4b).
Devil (/slanderer) = Satan = old serpent = huge dragon = deceiver (Rev. 12:9).
¤
¤ In ancient times, the dragon was not a dragon, but God's protective cherub, from which injustice was once found (Ezek. 28:11-19), Ezek. 28:13a, < You were in Eden, the garden of God.>
Then it and its angels were hurled down of Heaven to the earth (Rev. 12:7-9).

¤ In Eden, it led human race's first couple, Adam and Eve, astray. Although both fell differently. First, Eve had listened to the serpent (Gen. 3:1-6), 1Tim. 2:13-14, < For Adam was formed first, and then Eve. 14. And it was not Adam who was deceived, but the woman who was deceived and fell into transgression.>

Eve made a mistake by not inviting Adam to meet the serpent. For the woman is of the man. She is the glory of her husband, the representative of her husband, just as a man is the image and glory of God (cf. 1Cor. 11:7-8).

¤ The snake had suggested something strange to her and Adam would have been capable to see through it. Just as later the Lord Jesus was able to resist the Devil with the words "it is written" (Mat. 4:1-11).

Instead, Adam's mistake was that he listened to his wife, when he ate from the tree of the knowledge of good and evil. He knew that God had forbidden it (Gen. 3:17).

¤ The result was death, from which God's Son redeemed us (Rm. 5:12, etc. and Gal. 3:13).

Later, Jesus Christ didn't just resist the Devil completely. He was ready to sacrifice His Own Sinless Life, by which He justified and purified everyone who believes in Him (Titus 2:11-14).

¤

¤ The serpent had been the most developed animal of all animals, a human ape, that could even speak (cf. Gen. 3:1-5).

Regrettably, it had given itself to the dragon for use, something it could have resisted and denied. That is why God condemned it to go on its belly and to eat dust (cf. Gen. 3:14).

¤ Thus through the serpent the dragon had approached Eve and raped her (Rev. 12:9a). As a result, Cain was born as the first human child. On the other hand, seen from Eve's point of view, the birth of a child was even miraculous (Gen. 4:1).

¤ For mankind, it was the beginning of a sad struggle for the Truth, Gen. 3:15. <"…. And I will put enmity between you and the woman, and between your seed and her seed. He will crush your head, and you will strike his heel.">

In Heaven the dragon would have had nothing anymore to do. But after the sin fall it got again access to God by accusing people (Gen. 2:17; Rev. 12:10b), 'Did you not say that in the day a man eats of the tree of the knowledge of good and evil, he will surely die?'.

¤ According to the Jewish calendar, the waiting period of about four thousand years for the arrival of the specific seed of the woman began (Isa. 7:14; Mat. 1:18-23), Mat. 1:23, <"Behold, the virgin will be with child and will give birth to a son, and they will call Him Immanuel" (which means, "God with us").>

Then, by His death, Jesus Christ annulled the Devil who had the power of death (Heb. 2:14b).

¤ Once again the dragon was defeated and cast out (John 12:31; Rev. 12:7-10).

In the same way, every believer must be watching and firm in faith resist the Devil (1Pet. 5:8-9; Rev. 12:11).

Woman of Three Kingdoms

Shalom,
^ With Gentile believers God has had personal contacts. However, with the Jewish people His contact has been in addition with the entire people. Likewise, this people and their country have served as God's watch for the whole world.
The seeing of the birth of the state of Israel ('fig tree') in 1948 (and the becoming independent of many other 'trees') has shown that we live very close to the secret Presence of the Lord Jesus on the clouds (Mat. 24:32-44 and Lk. 21:29-33), Lk. 21:32, <Truly I say to you, this generation will not pass away until all things take place.>
With prayer of the saints, Bert

¤ In the beginning God's people of twelve tribes represented the Woman as seen in Heaven (3a§12, Rev. 12:1).
And halfway it should have continued to become the Bride of the Lord Jesus (Mat. 22:1-14).
¤ But many things went wrong. Firstly. Because of the idolatry of king Solomon and his wives, God tore this kingdom in two. Ten tribes were taken away (1Kings 11:29-39).
Later, because of extra fornication, God even let the kingdom of the 10 tribes be crushed (Hos. 1:1-9).
¤ Regrettably, the remaining people of the two tribes of Judah also opposed God, in demanding the crucifixion of His Son. That is why He divorced from that too (Mat. 21:33-46; 27:23).
Only a small number of the Jews had noticed the Messiah promised to them, and had followed Him (e.g. John 1:41).
¤ After the last separation, God turned away from the Jewish people to all the Gentile nations and peoples of the earth to look for a New Bride to His Son [a new kingdom, Lk. 17:21], 1Pet. 2:9-10, <But you are a chosen people, a royal priesthood, a holy nation, a people for God's own possession, …. 10. Once you were not a people, but now you are the people of God; once you had not received mercy, but now you have received mercy.>
When the last believer of the church ages has been found and God has taken all the members of this kingdom up in the first resurrection, the revival of the people of the 12 tribes will begin in the Greater tribulation time (Rev. 20:5), Rm. 11:25b-27, <A hardening in part has come to Israel, until the full number of the Gentiles has come in. 26. And so all Israel will be saved, as it is written: "The Deliverer will come from Zion; He will remove godlessness from Jacob. 27. And this is My covenant with them when I take away their sins.">

¤ First, 144,000, 12,000 of twelve tribes, comes to faith {Rev. 7:4-8 (7c§67₁14)}.
They are the firstfruits of the Jewish people {Rev. 14:(1-)4(-5)}.
¤ At the end of the time of the Greater Tribulation, all the rest of the Jews in Israel will meet their God. Sanctified one-third of the two-tribe-people of two thousand years ago {Zec. 13:6-9 and Mat. 26:31 (7d§67₁14)}.
However, since the crushing of the ten-tribe-people, many of their descendants have always lived among the Jewish people. With the word firstfruits, God is now speaking of the twelve-tribe-people. That's what He had even promised.
¤ Nowadays He is uniting the two people again into one kingdom/nation {Ezek. 37:15-28 (11b§19-22)}.
Likewise, at the very end, there are 12 representative tribes of the people of Israel found in the New Jerusalem (Rev. 21:12-13).
¤

¤ Every believer gets into fights. In the beginning it was seen between the first children, Cain and Abel. When both sons had grown into young men, Abel had chosen to become a keeper of sheep and Cain a tiller of the soil (Gen. 4:2b).
Then they offered a sacrifice to God. But God rejected Cain's gift, while He accepted Abel's gift (Gen. 4:3-5).
¤ Next, Cain showed his false character, as the apostle John later explained (Gen. 4:6-16), 1John 3:12, <…. Cain, who belonged to the evil one and murdered his brother. And why did Cain slay him? Because his own deeds were evil, while those of his brother were righteous.>
Cain represented people who had left from God's Instructions and Word. His sacrifice was beautiful. Regrettably it lacked the splashing atrocious ghastly animal blood (cf. Heb. 11:4).
¤ The story of Cain teaches that not all people have the same longing for God and the Truth. This was also noticed when Paul and Barnabas got almost all the inhabitants of the city of Antioch on the move, and the gospel was proclaimed with force. As many came to faith, as were appointed (Acts 13:48).
After the fall of Adam and Eve, finally Jesus was born. He was the seed promised to Eve as well as to Abraham and to every believer {3a§12, Gen. 3:15a (and Gen. 22:18, Gal. 3:16, Rev. 13:8b)}.
¤ Adam and Eve should have died on the same day they fell, but the All Knowing God of Love had another plan for salvation (Gen. 2:17), Gen. 3:21, <And the LORD God made garments of skin for Adam and his wife, and He clothed them.>
¤ In the Old Testament times, the shedding of blood (and the using of skins) of innocent animals had become a temporary solution to forgiveness. In that way had been covered up the nakedness of Adam and Eve, what had become visible (cf. Gen. 3:7).
¤ Then Christ came to give His Life, by what He became the Mediator of all (1Tim. 2:5-6; Heb. 9:11-15).
Everyone who believes in Him, is once and for all sanctified and made a part of His Covenant {3a§12, Heb. 10:(10-)16}.

Mankind's Two Most Beautiful Women

Shalom,
^ The church has for two thousand years represented the future Bride of Christ (Eph. 5:23-24a).
But another similar Bride is promised, represented by the people of the 12 tribes of Israel.
Of the New Jerusalem, called the Bride of the Lamb, both are found (§2a45, Rev. 21:12-14).
Prayer of them who know that God created all things, that is, all things (Isa. 66:1-2; Acts 7:50), Bert

¤ Every person around the world is called to be part of plans that God has predestined, among others personal plans (Eph. 2:10).
During seven revival periods people from all nations have been called (1a§1-3, Rev. 2:7; 2:11; etc.).
¤ It is extremely dangerous to fight with Satan against God's plans. Everyone is called to fight with the Holy Spirit against Satan's attacks, among others according to the promises of the book of Revelation (1a§1-3, Rev. 1:3), Rev. 22:10-11, <…. "Do not seal up the words of prophecy in this book, because the time is near. 11. Let the unrighteous continue to be unrighteous, and the vile continue to be vile; let the righteous continue to practice righteousness, and the holy continue to be holy.">
After the fall of mankind, the dragon/Satan/Devil had gotten again free access to Heaven before God (3a§12, Gen. 2:17).
¤ For example, in the time of Job Satan was in Heaven accusing him, and on earth only the killing of Job was forbidden (cf. Job 1:6-12).
On earth the devil was, when he personally tempted Jesus Christ after 40 days of fasting (Mat. 4:1-11).
¤ At the end of Jesus' ministry, His disciple Judas had noticed that his evil plan had been revealed to Jesus. But Judas hardened his heart and gave Satan room (John 13:1-27), John 13:27a, <And when Judas had taken the morsel, Satan entered into that one.>
The next day the same satanic spirit was found among the spiritual leaders of God's chosen people and of Pilate, the representative of the Roman state. Under the leadership of their leaders, the people demanded the crucifying of Christ and cried out (Mat. 27:15-26), Mat. 27:25, <"His blood be on us and on our children!">
¤
¤ It has cost a lot of blood. A long dangerous period among the Gentile nations began. Temporarily, God has set aside the Jewish people, while seeking a New Kingdom of born-again believers from all nations (3b§12, Lk. 17:21).

It is the Church, the Bride of the Lord Jesus, an incredibly beautiful, glorified Woman {Eph. 5:(23-)27}.

¤ Soon this Woman, the living and resurrected saints, will be raptured into heaven. It will take place with the secret Presence of our Lord in the clouds in the air {0c§Preface, 1The. 4:15b(-5:3)}.

All who have righteous acts, will be called to the Marriage Supper of the Lamb (Rev. 19:8-9).

¤

¤ One spiritual Kingdom has been saved and has reached the end goal (Rev. 12:10-12a).

But the first one, the twelve-tribes-kingdom, the Israel of today, is still on one's infancy, while a short terrible time is coming (3b§12, Zec. 13:6-9 and Mat. 26:31), Rev. 12:12b-13, <".... But woe to the earth and the sea; with great fury the devil has come down to you, knowing he has only a short time." 13. And when the dragon saw that he had been thrown to the earth, he pursued the woman who had given birth to the male child.>

¤ The following verse refers to the vision of the Seventy Week Years of the prophet Daniel, of which the concept of time and times and half a time contains a lot of symbolism and answers. Therefore, that prediction is treated in the following pages (3def§12), Rev. 12:14, <But the woman was given two wings of a great eagle to fly from the presence of the serpent to her place in the wilderness, where she was nourished for a time, and times, and half a time.>

In our time the Jewish people is back in a part of the land promised to them, which the dragon is very angry about (Gen. 15:18-21; Heb. 11:8-10), Rev. 12:15-16, <Then from the mouth of the serpent spewed water like a river to overtake the woman and sweep her away in the torrent. 16. But the earth helped the woman and opened its mouth to swallow up the river that had poured from the dragon's mouth.>

¤ On its own land, Israel has been able to defend itself against the dragon's water masses of men. As the waters are, Rev. 17:15, <.... peoples and multitudes and nations and tongues ....>

Soon the Jewish people will be ready to receive the rest of the land, also foretold by their prophet Ezekiel (Ezek. 47:13-23).

¤ Being in their own land didn't always help. When the Jewish people had participated in murdering God's Son, God had withdrawn His Blessing and forty years later Jerusalem was destroyed. Now first 144,000 Israelites are prepared for this (3b§12, Rev. 7:4-8).

At the end they are blameless spiritual virgins, who sing miraculous songs, follow the Lamb wherever He goes, do not lie, etc. Fully they represent the other incredibly beautiful Kingdom/Woman (Rev. 14:1-5).

The Seventy Year-Weeks for the Jewish People, Daniel §9

Shalom,
^ As a help to understand the twelfth chapter of Revelation, Daniel's prophecy of the year-weeks is reviewed.
Prayer of them who are determined in their mind not to defile themselves (Dan. 1:8), Bert

¤ About 605/606/616 BC the young Daniel was one of the first ones to be exiled to Babylon (Dan. 1:1-4).
There he became the king's counselor, prophet, supreme ruler of the regions and wise men, etc. And in the same way he was allowed to continue after the army of Media and Persia had conquered Babel (Dan. 1-8).
¤ After living in exile for almost 70 years, he realized that the prophet Jeremiah had prophesied that being in ruins of Jerusalem was to last seventy years. On this base he began to pray and confess the sins of the people (Dan. 9:1-20).
Thus came the angel of God, who gave him the word of the seventy year-weeks (Dan. 9:20-27), Dan. 9:24-27, <".... Seventy weeks/sevens are determined for your people and for your holy city, to finish transgression,1) and to make an end of sins,2) and to make reconciliation for iniquity,3) and to bring in everlasting righteousness,4) and to seal up vision and prophet,5) and to anoint the Most Holy.6) 25. And know therefore and understand: From the going forth of the word to restore and to build Jerusalem until the Messiah, the Prince, {there will be} seven weeks/sevens [the first stage of Jerusalem]. And sixty-two weeks/sevens, it will be built again. [The tenth and last, but not yet fully completed stage, when Jesus Christ arrives in Jerusalem as God's perfect temple (cf. John 2:19-21).] And with street and trench, and in times of distress. 26. And after the sixty-two weeks/sevens the Messiah will be cut off, and not for Himself. And the people of the prince who is to come, will destroy the city and the sanctuary; and his end {will be} with a flood. And unto the end {there will be} war; desolations {are} determined; 27. And he [the attacking prince] will strengthen a covenant with many {for} one week/seven, and {in} the midst of the week/seven he will cause Sacrifice and Offering to cease. And on the wing of abominations {will come} one who makes desolate, and even until that the consumption and what is determined, is poured on the one who makes desolate."
¤ The text has been translated on a word for word base. In addition, the beginning and end of the sentences have been if possible selected with help of the word 'and'.
The Hebrew language does not speak of a 'week' but of a '7-number', that is a period of 7 days or 7 years. Since Jeremiah had spoken of 70 years, it can be understood that we are talking about periods of years.
¤

¤ Shortly after the getting of this prophecy, King Cyrus of Persia asked the people of Judah to go to Jerusalem and to build the temple of the Lord God of Israel, in about 536/538 BC (Ezra 1:1-4).

The foundation of the temple was laid, but gradually opposition grew, and then the work stopped (Ezra 3:10; 4:24).

¤ Much later the temple was completed (Ezra 6:15).

After this, Ezra the priest came with many other ones, when he was commanded to put society and temple service in order {Ezra 7:(1-)11-26(-28)}.

¤ The word given to Daniel would say that 'From the going forth of the word to restore and to build Jerusalem', 'street and trench' would be built.

That text started to live among the Jewish people, when Nehemiah was made commander of the land of Judah. Very quickly under his leadership the wall and gates of Jerusalem were completed (Neh. 2:1-8; 6:15; 7:1).

¤ There are various alternatives for the year, when he would have gotten permission to leave, from 444 till 451 BC.

From this correct year could be counted, when Jesus Christ, 'the Messiah, the Prince' and the 'Sacrifice and Offering', would have begun His ministry. It would have been after 7 * (7 + 62) = 483 biblical years. According to God's time measure one month is 30 days and one year 360 days (cf. Rev. 11:2-3, 1260 days is 42 months).

¤ The corrected number of years would be 483 * 360 / 365.25 = 476 current years.

After that, the Ministry of Jesus Christ lasted about 7 * ½ = 3½ years before He was 'cut off'. 'And not for Himself', but for us, for all mankind.

¤ He was the true 'Sacrifice and Offering' of the temple service, who was crucified by Rome from the demands of the Jewish people (cf. Ex. 29:38-46; Dan. 8:13-14, 26; 11:31; 12:11; and Mat. 27:22).

That is why God after 7 + 62 + ½ year-weeks separated from His chosen people, and the clock of the Jewish people stopped. Still ½ year-week is waiting.

¤ Next 70 AD. the Roman army, led by General Titus, destroyed Jerusalem and its temple. Just before the end of the tenth and final stage. God had allowed 'one who makes desolate', to come.

A long period full of 'desolations' began. Later I will explain that for God the state of Rome and the church of Rome are the same entity, the same sixth head of the seven-headed beast (4a and 4b§1317).

¤ In this way, as 'one who makes desolate', it has raged throughout the last two thousand years. And there has been an evil 'strengthened 7-year covenant' between the 'one who makes desolate' and many, including the Jewish people, to persecute and kill Jesus Christ and His followers.

However, Israel is forced to leave the covenant, when the United States enters it and begins to rage {Dan. 9:27 (7b§67₁14)}.

Details of Year-Weeks' Prophesy, Daniel §9 and §12

Shalom,
^ Revelation 12 and the word of the year-weeks in the book of Daniel can be explained in many ways. However, an explanation must be found that is consistent with the entire Bible (2Pet. 1:20-21).
Prayer of them whose knowledge increases (Dan. 12:4), Bert

¤ The prophesy of the seventy year-weeks concerns the people of Daniel and Jerusalem (3d§12, Dan. 9:24):
1) 'To finish transgression'. The crucifixion of Jesus Christ, demanded by the Jewish people, is forgotten (Micah 7:18-20).
2) 'And to make an end of sins'. On the cross, Jesus Christ atoned for the sins of the whole world, including the sins of the Israelites (1John 2:2).
3) 'And to make reconciliation for iniquity'. In one day the whole nation will be born {Isa. 66:8 (7d§67₁14)}.
4) 'And to bring in everlasting righteousness.' The devil is captured, and the millennial sabbat time begins (Rev. 20:1-2), Hab. 2:14, <For the earth will be filled with the knowledge of the glory of the LORD as the waters cover the sea.>
¤
5) 'And to seal up vision and prophet'. In the end-time, vision and prophet will be understood (Dan. 12:8-10).
¤ The establishment of the State of Israel in 1948 was an important step {Mat. 24:32-35 and Lk. 21:29-33 (3b§12)}.
Next the recapture of Jerusalem took place, in 1967, within one generation (Lk. 21:32).
¤ It confirmed: Then the times of the Gentiles and the Christian churches were fulfilled (Lk. 21:24b (9k§89₁156)}.
Finally, those Christians who have served faithfully and wisely will be taken into heaven (Mat. 24:36-51).
¤ At that time the great angel/prince Michael will rise up and the Greater tribulation time will begin {0b§Introduction, Dan. 12:1(-3); Rev. 12:7-12a}.
The question is asked, when will the shattering of the hand/power of the holy people end? And among others is answered, {It will be for} a time, and times, and half {a time} {Dan. 12:(4-)6-7}.
¤ The same compound statement can be found in the Book Revelation (3c§12, Rev. 12:14).
At the previous page it was found that a logical connection to it is possible. The ministering period of Jesus Christ would have been a half year-week after 7 + 62 year-weeks. Taken together, it is 7 + 62 + ½ [time + times + half a time] = 69½ year-weeks. That would be God's own confirmation of this explanation!

¤ Jesus was the 'Messiah' / 'Sacrifice and the Offering', who was cut off. After that began a long era of the 'one who makes desolate' 'on the wing of abominations'. This process has continued until now and will at the end still continue 1335 days, Dan. 12:11-13, <".... And from the time of the removal of the daily sacrifice and of the setting up of the abomination of desolation, {there will be} 1,290 days. 12. Blessed is he who waits and reaches the end of the 1,335 days. 13. But as for you, go on your way until the end. You will rest, and will arise to your inheritance at the end of the days.">
It is the last half a time. First, two witnesses prophesy for 1260 days / 3½ years, before they are killed (Rev. 11:3).
¤ Then a similar time extension is found. After 3½ days they stand up on their feet and go up to heaven. And then there is a great earthquake, by what the purpose of the sixth trumpet will be fulfilled {Rev. 11:(9-)11-14 (9l§89₁156)}.
Both in the word of the seventy weeks and here is written about the same things. The 'daily sacrifice' is the same as the 'sacrifice and the offering'. Abomination is abomination. And the words desolation/desolate have the same root. In addition the word of the seventy year-weeks said, that the covenant was strengthened. But notice that this is an evil covenant. On the other hand, the texts of Dan. 8:10-14 and 11:30-34 spoke of the same things under the Holy Covenant between God and His chosen people. That was a different era, from the time of the Maccabees till the crucifixion of the Lord Jesus.
¤ Two thousand years ago the disciples of the Lord Jesus had among other things asked, when their temple would be destroyed {Mat. 24:1-3a (also 6h§6(8)10)}?
And He had answered that (Dan 9:27 ja 12:11), Mat. 24:15-21, <"So when you see standing in the holy place 'the abomination of desolation,' described by the prophet Daniel (let the reader understand), 16. then let those who are in Judea flee to the mountains. .... 21. For at that time there will be great tribulation, unmatched from the beginning of the world until now, and never to be seen again. ....">
¤ From the same kind of text in Luke can be learned, that there was spoken of the destroying by the Romans of Jerusalem and its temple, about forty years after the ministry of the Lord Jesus, Lk. 21:20-24a, <"But when you see Jerusalem surrounded by armies, you will know that her desolation is near. 21. Then let those who are in Judea flee to the mountains, (Etc.)">
And the text of Mark teaches that as the next thing Rome became the personification of these abominations and this one who makes desolate, Mrk. 13:14-19, <"So when you see the abomination of desolation standing where it should not be _let the reader understand_, then let those who are in Judea flee to the mountains. (Etc.)">
¤
6) 'And to anoint the Most Holy'. The 'one who makes desolate' will be destroyed and the other adversaries will be neutralized between the last 1290 and 1335 days {Rev. 11:11-14 (7be§67₁14 and 9l§89₁156)}.
The time has come to build a never-built temple according to the word of the prophet Ezekiel (Ezek. 40-48).

Revelation §12 in Light of the Seventy Year-Weeks

Shalom,
^ The seventy year-weeks of the book Daniel and its last chapter help us understand Revelation 12.
Prayer of them who are being built together into a dwelling place for God in His Spirit (Eph. 2:22), Bert

¤ Through His Son and those who believe in His Son, God has desired to call every person on earth to love in the same way, as He has loved mankind. Over the past two thousand years, many have been saved while at the same time they have been ready to sacrifice their life for the preaching of this Gospel (Mat. 28:18-20).

In addition we hear that in closed countries for example by dreams the Lord Jesus revealed Himself (John 5:17).

¤ With Christ in Heaven, they/we will reign in the soon starting millennial sabbat kingdom (Rev. 19-20).

After that, we will live forever with our God in the New Jerusalem (Rev. 21-22).

¤ But our Love Relationship needs to be in order. The apostle John sharply described the core of the challenge, 1John 4:20, <If anyone says, "I love God," but hates his brother, he is a liar. For anyone who does not love his brother, whom he has seen, cannot love God, whom he has not seen.>

In addition, God has His own hierarchy. To whom much has been given, much will be required (Lk. 12:48).

¤

¤ Verse Rev. 12:4a and 4b will be discussed later (9i§89$_1$156).

Next, I will take another look at the text of Revelation 12:5. The people of the land of Israel gave birth to a Son, the Lord Jesus, Who after His Service was taken to Heaven. But the majority of the Jews rejected the Messiah who was promised to them. That's why God turned away from His people and its seventy year-weeks' clock stopped.

¤ It will last until the Lord Jesus takes away His temporary Bride-church of all nations (Rm. 11:25b-26).

At that moment God will turn back to His former chosen people and it will enjoy God's Covenant and Grace as before (Rm. 11:23), Revelation 12:6, <And the woman fled into the wilderness, where God had prepared a place for her to be nourished for 1,260 days.>

¤ It had previously been found, that the statement 'Time and times and half a time' should be seen as a whole (3e§12, Rev. 12:14).

After that there would be left only half a time, 3½ years, 1260/1290/1335 days {3e§12, Dan. 12:(11-)12(-13)}.

¤

¤ The Invitation of the Gospel has been proclaimed to you, to me, and to every human child, regardless of nation, race, sex, status, age, etc. (Mat. 28:18-20).

Each of us must have been ready to seek and follow God's Will, as the Lord Jesus had chosen It for His own Life. In this way He had completely defeated the dragon, taken the sting out of its accusations, and redeemed all mankind (Heb. 10:7-10; and 3a§12, Rev. 12:7-10, 11)!

¤ In the same way, every believer is able to cast the dragon/Satan down (Lk. 10:17-20)!

Until Jesus takes His Gentile Bride up into Heaven (3c§12, Rev. 12:10-12a).

¤

¤ With the Rapture the Greater tribulation time begins, Rev. 12:(12b-)13, <And when the dragon saw that he had been thrown to the earth, he pursued the woman who had given birth to the male child.>

Two thousand years ago, the Jewish people were in their own country for 'time and times and a half', because Jesus Christ was coming to it (3c§12, Rev. 12:14).

¤ Now it will help them during the last half of the week. Therefore, the dragon then focuses on attacking the Messianic believers of/in Israel (Rev. 12:15-17a), Rev. 12:17a, <And the dragon was enraged at the woman, and went to make war with the rest of her children, who keep the commandments of God and hold to the testimony of Jesus.> Here we are talking about 144,000 messianic believers who will then come to faith. They live in obedience to the law, as did the Jewish believers in the early church (Acts 21:20-24).

¤ Most of the Jewish people in Israel today do not believe in God at all. They are in the land of their ancestors because there they are relatively safe. But the book Revelation shows that first it is the time for 144,000 Israelites. Previously they were sealed for their future spiritual work (Rev. 7:1-8).

The time of their coming to faith and their spiritual work begins when we, the believers of the Bride of Christ, are taken up into Heaven. We will then be seen before the Throne of God. All who had been filled with the Holy Spirit in their lives, did the Will of God, and endured all kinds of great tribulation pressures (Rev. 7:9-17).

~ ~ ~

First Beast

Shalom,
^ First, the dragon is hurled to the earth for the last time (3f§12, Rev. 12:(7---)13}.
Next, the believers will meet their Lord Jesus in His Presence (0c§Preface, 1The. 4:15b).
^ From that time the dragon will concentrate on persecuting the people of Israel, and especially the 144,000 messianic believers of the 12 tribes (3f§12; Rev. 12:(15-)17).
^ Among the Jewish people, the people of the two-tribes, there have always dwelled small numbers of citizens of the other 10-tribes. As well from many countries, smaller or larger ethnic groups of them have been found back.
Prayer of them who have already completely overcome the beast and its image and its mark (Rev. 20:4), Bert.

¤ This chapter continues with the same moment when the 12th chapter ends, with the beginning of the last half year-week of Daniel, Rev. 13:5, <To it [the beast] was given a mouth to speak arrogant and blasphemous words, and authority to act for 42 months.>
The dragon will no longer have a chance to visit Heaven and accuse believers. Now it stands between the promised land and the sea (3f§12, Rev. 12:10---17a), Rev. 12:17b, <And it [the dragon] stood on the shore of the sea.>
¤ Next, we see Satan's tool on earth. A copy or shadow of him, a brute giant monster, Rev. 13:1, <Then I saw a beast with ten horns and seven heads rising out of the sea. There were ten royal crowns on its horns and blasphemous names on its heads.>
The Devil-Satan-dragon gives this dragon-beast his destructive, shocking, and deadly powers (Rev. 12:9), Rev. 13:2b, <And the dragon gave to it [the beast] his power and his throne and great authority.>
¤ The meaning of the waters can be found in chapter 17. Of the same beast (and the prostitute sitting on it, Rev. 17:3) is spoken, Rev. 17:15b, <"The waters you saw, where the prostitute was seated, are peoples and multitudes and nations and tongues. ....">
Thus the beast (and prostitute) lives among peoples, multitudes, nations, and languages. And it was revealed, Rev. 17:9b-10, <The seven heads are seven mountains on which the woman sits. 10. There are also seven kings. Five have fallen, one is, and the other has not yet come; but when he does come, he must remain for only a little while.>
¤ Two thousand years ago, the sixth kingdom was the then world power, Rome, and the seventh kingdom will only last a short time. Therefore Rome's rule would last

relatively long. We learn from history that the Roman Empire became the Rome of the popes, as foretold in Rev. 13:3a, <One of the heads of the beast appeared to be mortally wounded. But the mortal wound was healed,>

As the Rome of the popes, it turned into a church described in the Bible as a woman (e.g., Eph. 5:23-33).

¤ God named the system in question Babylon the Great, the mother of the prostitutes and of the abominations of the earth (Revelation 17:5).

Next, the mystery of the prostitute and the beast was explained {cf. Rev. 17:(1-)7}.

¤ Instead of a beautiful pure virgin, the mother prostitute has been a sinful woman, Rev. 17:2, <".... The kings of the earth were immoral with her, and those who dwell on the earth were intoxicated with the wine of her immorality.">

The city of Rome was known at that time for being built on 7 hills. And it was foretold that as the prostitute it would be the same great city, that would rule over the kings/kingdoms of the earth: the Vatican city of the popes is a part of the city of Rome (cf. Rev. 17:7, 9, 18).

¤ The seven heads have represented seven dictatorial kingdoms, seven superpowers. One by one was/is conquering the entire civilization.

Throughout history representatives of the heads of the beast, rulers and popes, have been seen rising and declining, Rev. 17:8, <The beast that you saw—it was, and now is no more, but is about to come up out of the Abyss and go to its destruction. And those who dwell on the earth whose names were not written in the Book of Life from the foundation of the world will marvel when they see the beast that was, and is not, and yet will be.>

¤ The central purpose of the beast (and the prostitute) is to wage war against the saints and conquer them (Rev. 13:7).

But God has desired to choose such people as His servants, who do not bow to among others those political powers. Just like Jesus Christ. Satan offered all the kingdoms of the world and their splendor to Him too (Mat. 4:8-10).

¤

¤ A similar picture of the kingdoms of the world can be found in the dream of the statue of the king of Babylon (Dan. 2:19-45).

Rome has represented the iron legs of the statue, the 6th head of the beast.

¤ Copper belly and thighs were Alexander the Great of Greece, the 5th head of the beast.

The silver chest and arms were the rulers of Media and Persia, the 4th head of the beast.

¤ The golden head was Nebuchadnezzar, the third head of the beast.

The second head of the beast was possibly the pharaohs of Egypt, at some point (cf. e.g. Gen. 41-50).

¤ The first head of the beast was possibly the center of the tower of Babel, with among others Nimrod (Gen. 10:8-12; 11:1-9).

The 7th head of the beast will be dealt with the following times.

First and Second Beast

Shalom,
^ In Europe, two world wars broke out. The main opponents have had among others strong Roman Catholic background. It tells something about the false influence of the popes. In the case of France, this has been very clear. But also for Germany.
The beginning of the German state was the Holy Roman Empire founded in the 9th century. Regrettably, after the Reformation, it was not renewed. Up to the Peace of Westphalia in 1648, the majority of the German kings had persecuted many non-Roman Catholic believers away.
^ Here I still live in the same Europe. Much prayer I/we need of each other. Thanks for that!
With prayer of slaves(/servants) who fear their God (Rev. 19:5), Bert

¤ The sixth head of the first beast, the Roman Empire, has influenced world politics, first as the emperors of Rome. And after that, as the popes of Rome, when church' and political power have mixed together, Rev. 13:3-4, <One of the heads of the beast appeared to be mortally wounded. But the mortal wound was healed, and the whole world marveled and followed the beast. 4. They worshiped the dragon who had given authority to the beast, and they worshiped the beast, saying, "Who is like the beast, and who can wage war against it?">
The Roman Catholic Church represents about 50% of the Christians of the world. The majority of the wars could have been stopped if the pope had forbidden its church members to take part. Anyway, two World Wars were recently started here.
¤ Rev. 13:5-6, <The beast was given a mouth to speak arrogant and blasphemous words, and authority to act for 42 months. 6. And the beast opened its mouth to speak blasphemies against God and to slander His name and His tabernacle—those who dwell in heaven.>
The pope has blasphemed the name of God by speaking with His authority. The residence of the Holy Spirit would be in the Roman Catholic Church. Dead believers were blasphemed by saying they would be mediators.
¤ In chapter 17 this relationship of the prostitute Church with the political leaders was called fornication and it was told that the name of this prostitute, 'mother Babylon the Great', contains a secret (4a§1317, Rev. 17:2), Rev. 17:5, <And on her forehead a mysterious name was written: BABYLON THE GREAT, THE MOTHER OF THE PROSTITUTES AND OF THE ABOMINATIONS OF THE EARTH.>
With the Reformation, many daughters were born from this mother church, which at first were beautiful innocent children, where the Bible was respected and all sorts of

former Christian values were found back. But instead of continuing with separating the church from the state, new state churches were established.

¤

¤ References to the origin of the state which would probably represent the seventh head of the beast, can not be found directly in chapter 13. However, there is a lot between the lines. One might ask why Revelation 13 mentions another beast, another political power, even if all the nations of the world were already involved in the first one?

There is only one direct clue to it in the entire Book Revelation, Rev. 17:10b, <but when he [the seventh king] does come, he must remain for only a little while.>

¤ The first beast had risen from the sea, that is, from peoples and multitudes and nations and tongues, in which and by which it has ruled the whole world (4a§1317, Rev. 17:15b).

But the origin of the second beast is different. It has a more solid foundation than humans. It came from the earth, Rev. 13:11, <Then I saw another beast rising out of the earth. This beast had two horns like a lamb, but spoke like a dragon.>

¤ What would it mean to come from the earth? Previously, a connection was already found to the land of Israel, to God's land. As long as the people of Israel was a part of the Word of God, what was promised for that time, their own land would help to stop Satan's attacks (3c/3f§12, Rev. 12:15-16).

The earth also provides a better base than waters on which a life worthy of God's kingdom can be built (cf. Mat. 7:24).

¤ There is another way to see that the second beast does not represent just brute power. From the outside, this beast even looks good, a 'Lamb'. Almost like the Lamb of God, almost like Christ. But still it is not the same Christ, for 'it spoke like a dragon'.

It has 'two horns', two sources of power, political and spiritual power. Thus it would be the world state of the coming antichrist (!).

¤ So it can be associated with the antichrist who will settle himself in the temple of the church of Jesus Christ in the last days (Eph. 2:21-22), 2 Thess. 2:3b-4, <for it [that day] will not come until the rebellion/apostasy occurs and the man of lawlessness—the son of destruction—is revealed. 4. He will oppose and exalt himself above every so-called god or object of worship. So he will seat himself in the temple of God, proclaiming himself to be God.>

The Greek word 'naos' does not speak of a temple building, although many Bible teachers say this. It speaks of the room or pedestal inside the temple where the statue of God stood. The place for God, where this opposer will settle. Once Jesus' beloved ones are taken up, there will be no longer an obstacle for him. Then he will take over the remaining system of churches (1The. 4:14-17; 2The. 2:7).

Second Beast and Image of First Beast

Shalom,
^ Last time I wrote about the influence of the Roman Catholic Church in Europe. The development of similar influences in the United States is now being discussed. As well, more and more connections can be noticed between them two.
Prayers of them who have long white linen robes (Rev. 3:5; 3:18; 4:4; 7:14; 16:15; 19:14), Bert

¤ I continue with the second beast. I'm going to provide evidence that the United States and this beast are one and the same thing. Later I will deal with when and in what way it becomes the seventh head of the first beast {Rev. 12:13 (6k§6(8)10)}, Rev. 13:12, <And it [the second beast] exercised all the authority of the first beast and caused the earth and those who dwell in it to worship the first beast, whose mortal wound had been healed.>

The United States and its presidents have been a Protestant state since the beginning. However, at an increasing rate, it has begun to consult the represents of the sixth head of the first beast, the popes of Rome.

¤ Since president Eisenhower's visit in 1959, every subsequent president has visited the pope. In addition, John F. Kennedy was the first Roman Catholic president in the 1960s. And in 1984, the United States established full diplomatic relations with the Vatican City. Kennedy knew, that Protestant Americans did not want to vote for him because of his religion. That is why he had promised to leave it outside his politics. The last president, Biden, on the other hand, is the second Catholic president who has a very free understanding of his religion. Openly he has used Roman Catholic greetings and concepts.

¤ With regard to the State of Israel, there is a big difference in attitude between former president Trump and the other last presidents of the USA. Trump somehow acknowledged Israel's right to exist in areas it once conquered in wars, because it was attacked and threatened with destruction. This recognizing is normal and based on international law.

The Abraham Accords showed, that even peace with Islamic states is possible without a so-called 'peace' solution for the Palestinians.

¤

¤ Rev. 13:13, <And it [the second beast] performed great signs to cause even fire from heaven to come down to earth in the presence of the people.>

As a state, the USA has been a pioneer in the development of modern weapons. For example since World War II, it has been the world's highest developed state. It fulfills the best of all the states in the world this verse.

¤

¤ Rev. 13:14-15, <Because of the signs that were given to it {[to the second beast]} to perform on behalf of the first beast, it deceived those who dwell on the earth, telling them to make an image to the beast that had been wounded by the sword and yet had lived. 15. It [The second beast] was permitted to give breath to the image of the first beast, so that the image could speak and cause all who refused to worship it to be killed.>

The picture what is made of the beast, must show something of the current stage of the first beast at that time. That is, something of the sixth head of the beast that recovered as the popes' city of Rome (4a§1317, Rev. 13:3a).

¤ This papal Rome was described as a great prostitute, as God saw it (4a§1317, Rev. 17:1-7).

It was also said that this Babylon the Great is the mother of prostitutes and of the abominations of the earth. She gave birth to many Protestant churches who would later follow their mother's fornication ways (4b§1317, Rev. 17:5).

¤ Similarly, the second beast is represented by the Protestants who, after the Reformation, had left Roman Catholic-influenced Europe and had begun a new life based on the Bible in the United States.

Regrettably, the new churches and congregations have gradually returned to the same lifeless organizations with all sorts of patterns and traditions as the mother church. Everyone is forced to believe what is commonly approved. Access to the pulpit requires a church membership or education card. A personal view is not accepted. Then you risk to be killed spiritually (by ignoring you). And soon you will really be 'killed', when the image of the beast is given a 'spirit' and its worship is demanded.

¤ In 1948, the World Council of Churches (WCC) was established. The organization's website states that the group's goal is Christian unity and that most of the founding churches of the WCC were European and North American. The Protestants of the United States were the largest and most influential group internationally. Such an image of the beast was inspired and started.

When the Bride Church is raptured to Heaven and the time of the Greater Tribulation begins, the president of the United States will give it the opportunity to speak on behalf of all the Protestants. Then to it is given breath. Later that will be dealt with (8d§89₁156).

¤ At the same time, the president in question is accepted as the leader of the World Council, by which he will seat himself in the temple of God as the leader of all Protestants in the world {4b§1317, 2The. 2:(3b-)4, 7}.

But instead of being led by the Holy Spirit, he himself makes decisions as God (2The. 2:4)!

Second Beast and Mark of First Beast

Shalom,
^ The second beast in Revelation 13 would be the United States. All kinds of confirmations were found with the previous verses. Now the review is continued with the remaining verses.
Prayer of them who want to come out of organized worship to avoid its sins and scourges {Rev. 18:4-5 (10a§18)}, Bert

¤ Revelation 13:16-18, <And it [the second beast] required all people small and great, rich and poor, free and slave, to receive a mark/engraving on their right hand or on their forehead, 17. so that no one could buy or sell unless he had the mark/engraving—the name of the beast or the number of its name. 18. Here is a call for wisdom: Let the one who has insight calculate the number of the beast, for it is the number of a man, and that number is 666.>
What would be the ENGRAVED MARK of the beast? And why would the United States adopt it?
¤ This text speaks of marking the entire U.S. population and possibly many other populations with a monetary mark.
Why is it happening and in what way could that turmoil be triggered?
¤
¤ After World War II, the US dollar became the world's dominant global currency after remaining the only gold-backed currency.
Then in the 60s, the United States sold a lot of its gold assets.
¤ Still, the dominance of the dollar continued. But the country's debt rate has increased dramatically. This development and major events since 1929 can be found in the list, https://www.thebalance.com/national-debt-by-year-compared-to-gdp-and-major-events-3306287
The total debt of the US by the end of 2022 was 31.42 * 1012 dollars, or 123 percent of its Gross Domestic Product.
¤ It also says that according to the World Bank, long-term debt of more than 77% of GDP slows economic growth.
Thus, the collapse of the U.S. economic system for some unforeseen reason is no longer mere speculation. At the same time, it would affect global trade and cripple world's business. In that case a payer of the debts is sought. And the text in question states that he will be found. Next, everyone will be helped to take his mark. But God has also warned that that solution involves idolatry, what He does not allow. Because of that, at the end you will go straight to hell (Rev. 14:9-11)!
¤

¤ Who would be this payer, what would be the NAME OF THE BEAST? On the previous pages it has already been indicated that Rome, and in particular the Rome of the popes, is still the sixth head of the first beast. As long as the second beast has not yet become the seventh head of the beast (e.g. 4b§1317).

When that huge monetary crisis arises, the papal Rome could provide a revolutionary solution. It would pay off the debts of the dollar and the paper money of many other Western countries, just as all Western countries depend a lot on each other. However, anyone who subsequently wishes to use this renewed money will have to accept the NAME OF THE BEAST or the NUMBER OF THE NAME OF THE BEAST either on his forehead or on his hand.

¤ Does this idea match all the details? The NUMBER (OF THE NAME) OF THE BEAST would be the NUMBER OF A MAN, just as the first beast and the pope represent the same thing. And its number would be 666 (Rev. 13:18).

In practice, the number 666 can be found in the names of many people. But in this end time there is only one who has been a representative of the Christian Church that has governed the world in more than a thousand years, the pope. A direct reference to the name of the popes can be found in the title of the popes 'VICARIUS FILII DEI', which is the language of ancient Rome. It means 'Deputy of the Son of God'. It is an incredible title. Instead of the Lord Jesus, a man should be worshiped.

¤ The name is used in the form of 'Vicar of Christ' as one of the qualities of the pope. Read, for example, what the Roman Catholic magazine teaches. The pope is / would be the Vicar of Christ, the Deputy of Christ:

https://www.catholiceducation.org/en/culture/catholic-contributions/papal-tiara.html

¤ When you sum the Latin letters of the VICARIUS FILII DEI name, the result is 666. Latin letter values are V = 5, i = 1, C = 100, D = 500, and L = 50. Letters without a numeric value (a, r, f, s, and e) are counted as zero. Thus 5 + 1 + 100 + 1 + 5 + 1 + 50 + 1 + 1 + 500 + 1 = 666.

¤

¤ The BEAST NUMBER 666 refers to a very powerful system. It is the political system that governs the modern world, the beast of the seven heads, as Satan offered it to Jesus Christ (4a§1317, Mat. 4:8-10).

On the earth it has a great deal of power. But not as much as the God of the Creation, 777. In this way Jesus Christ defeated the dragon and got the keys of death and hell (3a§12, Gen. 3:15; and Rev. 1:18).

¤ Last time I discussed the fact that recently the United States has been approaching the popes in Rome.

The pope's role in paying of the debts should be understood as a consequence by which he gains recognition and power.

Background of the Popes' Title "VICARIUS FILII DEI"

Shalom,
^ Since 4.2020, the current pope Francis has suddenly, without any explanation, declared that he is (only) the bishop of Rome. In 2013, he had become pope. However, the contents of the pope's titles speak louder than the pope's words. At one time it was thus believed, and proclaimed, and affirmed. And the following Roman Catholic source provides a good explanation, link, https://catholicherald.co.uk/did-pope-francis-really-drop-the-vicar-of-christ-title/:
".... All of the other titles "are understood to be tied historically to the title of bishop of Rome because at the moment he is designated by the conclave to guide the church of Rome, the one elected acquires the titles tied to this nomination." ...."
Prayer of them who bow their knees only to the Father in Heaven (Eph. 3:14), Bert

¤ Basically, each pope has the following list of eight titles.
It is the official list of papal titles in the order they were/are given in the annual 'Annuario Pontificio'. For the titles in question, I have given (biblical) reviews and confirmations.
¤
1. The Bishop of Rome
The Roman Catholic Church claims that the apostle Peter had been the first pope.
<a. However, not a single document from that time has been found that Peter would have visited Rome.
<b. The apostle(s) Paul (and Barnabas) worked among the pagan peoples, but the apostle Peter only among the circumcised (cf. Gal. 2:7-9).
¤
¤ At one time, the empire of Rome turned into a spiritual power (4a§1317, Rev. 13:3a).
>c. The Roman Catholic Church is a prostitute church led by popes which is not faithful to its spouse, Jesus Christ. It can be found in the Bible as a woman/prostitute sitting on the seven hills of the old city of Rome (4a§1317, Rev. 17:(1-)7, 9, 18).
¤
2. Vicar of Jesus Christ / Deputy of Jesus Christ
<a. There is only one mediator between God and men, the man Christ Jesus (1Tim. 2:5).
<b. The pope is not the Holy Representative of God. The Holy Spirit came as the Vicar of the Lord Jesus (John 16:7).
<c. If you want to meet the Pope, you must bend your knee before him and call him Holy Father or Your Holiness. It is unforgivable idols' worshiping (Ex. 20:1-5; Mat. 23:9; Rev. 21:8; 22:15).
¤

¤ The pope would be the VICARIUS FILII DEI / DEPUTY OF THE SON OF GOD. This title was discussed at the former page (4d§1317, Rev. 13:(16-)17-18).
>d. There is only one Son of God, Jesus Christ, of whom every person should be a witness (Lk. 24:44-48).
> e. One does not get power after becoming pope. But when he/she has received the gift of the Holy Ghost (Acts 1:8; 2:38).
¤

3. Successor of the Prince of the Apostles

<a. In fact, Paul would be the chief apostle of the apostles of Jesus' time. The Holy Spirit did more work with him than with the other ones (e.g. 1Cor. 15:9-10; 2Pet. 3:15-16).
¤
>b. Another successor of the prince of the apostles could be compared to a false prophet (e.g. Rev. 16:13).
>c. The false prophet will be thrown directly into the fiery lake at the end of the Greater tribulation period (Rev. 19:20; 20:10).
>d. The guideline would not be what the pope or his church says, but what God's Word says (Gal. 1:8; Rev. 22:18-19).
> e. The church is not the Teacher of God's Word, but the Holy Spirit (John 16:13).
¤

4. Supreme Pontiff of the Universal Church

<a. Christ is the Head of everything, and likewise the Head of the Church and every believer (Col. 1:13-19).
¤
>b. The Roman Catholic Church claims that its own name is identical with the original universal [=Catholic] Church from which all other denominations descended. With this claim and definition God is fully of the same opinion. The universal church would be Babylon the Great, the mother of prostitutes and of the abominations of the earth (4bc§1317, Ilm. 17:5).
¤

5. Primate of Italy

¤

6. Archbishop and Metropolitan of the Province of Rome

¤

7. Sovereign of Vatican City State

¤

8. Servant of the Servants of God

~ ~ ~ ~ ~ ~

5a§6(8)10

Right and Wrong Church

Shalom,
^ The Seals are the most central and deepest secrets of the Book Revelation and the Bible (Rev. 6 and 8:1).
The sealing of those seals God had commanded (Rev. 10:3-4).
It is impossible to accept or to think, that the meanings of the seals can be found with the help of human wisdom. They cannot be explained in a way that another interpreter of the Bible says this, but the opinion of another interpreter must also be taken into account. God has sharply opposed it already in general, 2Pet. 1:19-21,
<We also have the word of the prophets as confirmed beyond doubt. And you will do well to pay attention to it, as to a lamp shining in a dark place, until the day dawns and the morning star rises in your hearts. 20. Above all, you must understand that no prophecy of Scripture comes from one's own interpretation. 21. For no such prophecy was ever brought forth by the will of man, but men spoke from God as they were carried along by the Holy Spirit.>
^ The last book of the Bible, the Revelation of God / Jesus Christ, had come directly from God and had been confirmed by the apostle John (1a§1-3, Rev. 1:1, 2).
John had been then the last living disciple of Jesus. At the same time God's Own Words closed the Book Revelation, the New Testament and the Bible (1a§1-3, Rev. 22:18-19).
In the same way, Jesus Christ had confirmed and closed the Old Testament (Mat. 5:17-20).
^ Only within the framework of the Bible can one expect some addition or some cancellation. That is, only in the way what God has announced in advance and what is in harmony with His entire work of creation. In that frame, dealing with the secrets of the Seals has been challenging and blessed.
Here God is our Leader and Father, and we are all equal sisters and brothers (cf. Rev. 1:9), Bert

¤ From the Bible, we know exactly how the first original church was founded and how God expressed Himself among it. Thus, what the church was at Pentecost is a type. And there is no other example. What God did at Pentecost, He must do until the church ages end. What the unchanging God with his unchanging ways did in the beginning, He will do until it is done for the last time (Eccl. 3:14-15).

The church and its messengers can change. But God and His ways never change (Heb. 13:8).

¤ In the beginning, on Pentecost, the believers had everything. The pure Word of God, the Power of the Spirit, the gifts of the Holy Spirit, etc. It was not organized by men, but led by the Holy Spirit. Many times it was hated, despised, harassed, and persecuted until death. But still it was faithful to God. It remained in the pattern given by the original Word. It had been the first revival age of the churches (1a/1b§1-3, Rev. 1:20).

To the first church age of Ephesus belonged the star messenger Paul. He was unorganized, led by the Spirit, and compared to all other apostles, he did by God's Grace the most spiritual work (1Cor. 15:10), Gal. 1:1, <Paul, an apostle—sent not from men nor by man, but by Jesus Christ and God the Father, who raised Him from the dead—>

¤ Paul was absolutely faithful to the Word. His ministry took place in the power of the Spirit, thus bringing forth the spoken and written Word. It was the ministry given to him by God, that produced visible fruit. It would be good for other messengers of the churches to strive to imitate the apostle Paul (cf. 1Cor. 4:15-16).

The apostolic age is not over. The promise of power is until God stops calling (Acts 1-28), Acts. 2:38-39, <Peter replied, "Repent and be baptized, every one of you, in the name of Jesus Christ for the forgiveness of your sins, and you will receive the gift of the Holy Spirit. 39. This promise belongs to you and your children and to all who are far off—to all whom the Lord our God will call to Himself.">

¤

¤ The word teaches that already in the first churches a wrong spirit entered (1John 2:18-19).

But God does not abandon His own or allow them to fall into total error. The scriptures clearly say that the elect cannot be deceived, Mat. 24:24, <For false christs and false prophets will appear and perform great signs and wonders that would deceive even the elect, if that were possible.>

¤ So what? There is a right Church and a wrong church.

The false church always tries to steal the right church's place and claims that it and not the elect is right and genuine. The wrong tries to destroy the right (e.g. 3John 1:10).

¤

¤ The fundamental error, or the errors that crept into the first church and which were announced in the books Acts of the apostles, Revelation and in the letters, become more and more visible in the successive church ages.

In the church of the end time, there will be a total darkening of the truth (1b§1-3, Rev. 3:14-22).

End-Time Church Age

Shalom,
^ God has predicted the future. This is how it is going to happen. Believers just have to be constantly awake and e.g. to study God's Word. So we are able to be in harmony. And we do not oppose what is constantly progressing around us.
Prayer of them, who work out their salvation with fear and trembling (Phili. 2:12), Bert

¤ There have been two chains of events throughout the era of the churches. After the revival age of the Ephesian church, three other weaker and weaker revival ages followed, during which knowledge of God's Word and awareness of a healthy Christian life decreased all the time. The darkness became darker and darker. At the end there was literally a long dark age (1b§1-3, Rev. 2:5).

After that, another development chain began with the Reformation. Under Luther's leadership believers were unified and became stronger. Many strange teachings of the Church of Rome were exposed. In this church age of Sardis, the Protestants united against the Roman Catholic structures of power. Next, in the Philadelphian church age in the English-speaking world the Gospel was powerfully spread, and a pure and humble Christian way of life developed.

¤ In the end time church age of Laodicea, spiritual gifts were found back on a large scale, and there was a lot of evangelizing in the streets and persistent prayer meetings. But gradually the spiritual life according to God's perfect Will changed to God's permitted Will.

Today, almost every church believes that they have the only (or almost) true and correct teaching, faith and way of life. They/We are so blind that they/we do not even realize that they/we are blind (Rev. 3:17).

¤ We live very close to the Presence of the Lord Jesus in the clouds. Many and deep truths have been rediscovered. But they are of no use if the Giver of Life is no longer involved (1b/1c§1-3, =), Rev. 3:20, <"…. Behold, I stand at the door and knock. If anyone hears My voice and opens the door, I will come in and dine with him, and he with Me. ….">

There is a lot of confusion about this verse because so many use it in personal evangelism. Jesus would be knocking at the door of every sinner's heart for entrance. Thus it could be said that if the sinner opens the door, the Lord would enter. But this verse is not speaking to individual sinners. This entire message is a summary for all the churches of that church age, Rev. 3:22, <"…. He who has an ear, let him hear what the Spirit says to the churches.">

¤ This is a message to the believers of the churches of the last age. This is the condition of the church of Laodicea as its end approaches.

The Spirit tells us where Jesus is. Christ has left the church. It is the logical result or end. God's Word has been put aside for creed, the Holy Spirit deposed for popes, bishops, presidents, counsellors, etcetera, and the Saviour set aside for work programs, or joining a church (congregation), or accepting some kind of church system. This is the apostasy! This is the falling away! This is the open door for the antichrist!

¤

¤ The age of the church of Laodicea is the harvest time (Rev. 14:14-20), Rev. 14:15b, <"Swing Your sickle and reap, because the harvest hour has come; and the crop of the earth is ripe.">

Those who cause the wheat and the weeds to ripen must come forward. Weeds ripen very quickly under their corrupt teachers who turn people away from the Word (Mat. 13:24-30 ja 37-43).

¤ The wheat must also ripen. For that, God must send a prophet-messenger with a ministry confirmed by the Holy Spirit so that the elect could receive him. He turns the hearts of the fathers and forefathers of the Jewish people to Jesus and his early apostles, and the hearts of the generations of the Christian children to Jesus and his early apostles (1d§1-3, Mal. 4:6).

The true church would again be the bride it was on the day of Pentecost. Therefore, the dynamic power must also return to the church, as believers in many places sense in their spirit. They have cried out to God for the same outpouring as in the first century and many have begun to speak in tongues and manifest the gifts of the Spirit.

¤ The spirit of the antichrist is in many false christs / anointed ones of this last day (5a§6(8)10, Mat. 24:24).

God would have anointed them for this last day. But God's Word says they are false christs (anointed ones). They claim to be prophets, but they are not one with the Word. They have added to it or taken something away (Rev. 22:18-19).

¤ Now we can see why there were two vines. Now we can see why Abraham had two sons; one according to the flesh (which persecuted Isaac) and the other according to the promise (Gal. 4:22-31).

Elect of God, be on your guard! Please investigate carefully! Be careful! Work out with fear and trembling your salvation! Trust in God and be strong in His Power!

Prophetic Background

Shalom,
^ The Bible is God's infallible Word. And God is wiser than us humans.

Someone may believe that the best way to believe in God and his Word is the belief that one should live without explanations. You will automatically see over time what everything means. In contrast, God's revelation speaks that He will reveal the secret and the future to his prophets, Amos 3:1-15, <Hear this word that the LORD has spoken against you, ... 2. "Only you have I known from all the families of the earth; therefore I will punish you for all your iniquities." .... 7. Surely the Lord GOD does nothing without revealing His plan to His servants the prophets. .... 15. I will tear down the winter house along with the summer house; the houses of ivory will also perish, and the great houses will come to an end," declares the LORD.>

Prayer of them who take care of the servants of the Lord Jesus, even now {(Mat. 24:45-46(-51)}, Bert

¤ I have my own explanations too. But I'm not the prophet of the end time, so I don't want to lock my own thoughts. I try to be ready to listen to other believers. The Book Revelation states, that the secret of God would get it's fulfillment in the time of the seventh messenger/angel, Rev. 10:7, <But in the days of the voice of the seventh angel, when he is about to sound {the} trumpet, the mystery of God shall also be completed, according to the gospel {that} He declared to His servants the prophets.>

Who would this messenger/angel be? Could he be the prophet of our end times (cf. 1d§1-3)?

¤ He would be a messenger on earth. Just as an angel is seen a little earlier, who came down from heaven and placed his right foot on the sea and his left on the earth (Rev. 10:1-2).

And on earth this messenger blows the trumpet.

¤ There are also trumpet angels in heaven. But he cannot be one of them, because in Heaven they received trumpets (Rev. 8:2).

If he is one of them, he should have died first. That would be an impossible combination.

¤

¤ Of which things could the blowing of a trumpet on earth tell? Paul has a good answer, 1Cor. 14:8-9, <Again, if the trumpet sounds a muffled call, who will prepare for battle? 9. So it is with you. Unless you speak intelligible words with your tongue, how will anyone know what you are saying? You will just be speaking into the air.>

During the Old Testament, the trumpet was used for example to gather God's people, or set the camps in motion. There was both an alarm call and an ordinary call. Also it could have possibly set God in motion. And there was a summoning call for the leaders (Numb. 10:1-10).

¤ It means that the messenger in question calls his fellow believers to spiritual warfare. In addition to that, he was called the seventh messenger/angel. In this way he could be the messenger of the seventh church (Rev. 3:14).

¤

¤ Previously it was discussed that the 7 churches of the Book Revelation would be 7 revivals (cf. 1a§1-3).

And their 7 messengers/angels would be the star messengers of each age (1b§1-3, Rev. 1:20).

¤ The apostle Paul would have been the star messenger of the first church age, of Ephesus. And so on.

The messenger of the Laodicean church would represent the star messenger of the revival of our end time.

¤ It is also known that the prophet Elijah of our end time is a prophet on earth.

He will appear before the great and terrible Day of the LORD (1d§1-3, Mal. 4:1-6).

¤

¤ The seventh church in the Book of Revelation, Laodicea, would represent the last revival and age of the churches. After it the horrors of the Greater tribulation time begin. Though firstly all the believers of the Bride Church would be taken up into Heaven (3c§12, Rev. 19:9).

In other words, in the same end time of the churches, these leading and significant messengers would live. Thus they could be one and the same man of God. Are there other common features and confirmations?

¤ Outside of the churches of the Laodicean church age its messenger should possibly be searched for and found. Just like John the Baptist, anointed with the spirit of Elijah, two thousand years ago. He was not found in the city of Jerusalem, or in its temple, or in some synagogue, but in the wilderness of Judea (Mat. 3:1).

And notice, even Jesus' disciples had not recognized him (Mat. 17:9-13)!

¤ He was the third Elijah-spirit prophet after the prophet Elisha (2 Kings 2:9-12).

 The first Elijah-prophet had alone been able to oppose the leaders of God's people (e.g. 1Kings 18:16-46)!

¤ The same challenge to recognize the Elijah of our time, the fourth Elijah-spirit prophet, would be now. Who works or worked in the same way? And does/did this person really meet the Lord Jesus, when 'the mystery of God shall also be completed' (see above)?

With these questions will be dealt with the next four times.

(And the fifth Elijah-prophet would be one of the two witnesses {Rev. 11:(5-)6 (7a§67₁14)}).

Backgrounds in the Book Revelation

Shalom,
^ From the church ages come the Seals, from the Seals the Trumpets, and from the Trumpets the Bowls. One creates light for the other.
Finally, the entire Revelation unfolds wide-angled in front of our wondering eyes. And we, who have been uplifted and purified, are prepared by the Spirit for His glorious appearing, so our Lord and Savior, the only One True God, Jesus Christ (Rev. 1:1aa).
Prayer of the servants/slaves of Jesus Christ (Rev. 1:1ab), Bert:
Such a thing must be absorbed as the apostle John had to do:

¤ Revelation chapters 1-3 are the chapters of the seven churches.
After that, Heaven opens in the chapters 4 and 5. There is seen the moment when the Scroll Sealed with Seven Seals was passed to the Lamb, the Lord Jesus Christ, to open the Seals.
¤ After that, only of the first six seals is seen symbols (Rev. 6).
¤
¤ Next, the sealing of 144,000 Israelites is told about (3f§12, Rev. 7:1-8).
It will end when the Church of the Bride is raptured, and the time of the Greater Tribulation begins. Thus we see the reception of the raptured saints before the Throne of God (3f§12, Rev. 7:9-17).
¤ In the next chapter, the Lamb opened the Last Seal of the Scroll seen in Revelation 5, Rev. 8:1, <When he [the Lamb] opened the seventh seal, there was silence in heaven for about half an hour.>
The silence of half an hour is a secret period when no one speaks in Heaven. A very special event, because silence is not normal in Heaven (cf. Rev. 4:8).
¤ In the same way, nothing has been announced of the day of the Coming/Presence of the Lord Jesus in the air. Even Jesus Himself did not know when it would happen (Mat. 24:36-44; 1The. 4:15-17).
Later, the apostle Paul said that the becoming imperishable of the Bride believers is a secret that happens when the last, i.e. the seventh, trumpet sounds (1Cor. 15:51-52; Rev. 11:15-19).
¤ Similarly, at first only the symbols of the first six trumpets are found (Rev. 8:2-9:21).
¤
¤ At the beginning of the book Revelation, Jesus Christ was seen on earth when He met the apostle John (Rev. 1:9-20).
In Heaven He had been since his Ascension. And after this Appearance He was again in Heaven.

¤ Then in the 10th chapter a similar Appearance is announced (Rev. 10:1-6a), Rev. 10:1-2, <Then I saw another strong angel/messenger coming down from heaven, wrapped in a cloud, with a rainbow above his head. His face was like the sun, and his legs were like pillars of fire. 2. He held in his hand a small scroll/book, which lay open. He placed his right foot on the sea and his left foot on the land.>
The Lord Jesus is described many times with clouds (e.g. Rev. 1:7).
¤ The rainbow can also be found at the Throne of God, where the Lord Jesus sits (Rev. 3:21 and 4:3).
Jesus' feet are like bronze glowing in a furnace and his face is like the sun (Rev. 1:15-16).
¤ The angel/messenger in question is the Lord Jesus Christ again. He had been the Only One Who had been Worthy to receive the Scroll out of God's Hands and open It (Rev. 5).
The seven-sealed Scroll is to every person and to all nature a promise of God's Plan of Salvation, the Plan of Redemption, the Secret of Redemption (cf. Rev. 5:9-10).
¤ He swore by Him who lives forever and ever and has created everything. It is God the Father in this place, just as God the Father and Jesus Christ are the same God (Rev. 10:6b).
For example, of God is spoken in the same way at the beginning of the Bible (Gen. 1:1).
¤ The messenger of the seventh church could be at the same time present on earth when the Angel in question appears (cf. 5c§6(8)10, Rev. 10:7).
This messenger should be a prophet, who even would know beforehand that he would see Jesus Christ. As John the Baptist had known that, two thousand years ago (John 1:33-34).
¤ Thus before the Rapture the Elijah of our time would meet the Lord Jesus Christ.
¤
¤ The seven-sealed Scroll should be the most important thing for every person in this world. Likewise, the apostle John was supposed to absorb it (Rev. 10:8-11), Rev. 10:9b, <"Take it and eat it," he said. "It will make your stomach bitter, but in your mouth it will be as sweet as honey.">
When you live by the gospel of Christ crucified, your Redeemer, it's hard to digest. Your stomach gets bitter. Everybody is against you. You are called crazy and a holy roller. When the battle is on, it's hard. But when this is over and you are testifying of the glory of God, it is sweet in the lips.
¤ In your mouth, it's as sweet as honey. Your name was paid for by the Blood of the Lamb that was slain (Rev. 13:8)!

Seven Angels of Heaven (1): Introduction

Shalom,
^ The next sermon belongs to the process of the opening of the seals.
I am writing about him who has told in more than a thousand recorded sermons how his whole life was prepared for the opening of those seals: William Marrion Branham (1909-1965).
^ Beginning in 1946, he held big campaigns throughout the United States.
In the fifties he also campaigned all over the world.
^ God had given him special gifts, with which he had been better able to pray for the sick and to see the thoughts of a person's heart. Later the Holy Spirit compared the first gift to small birds, or the first pull, and the second gift to larger birds, or the second pull. Here we are told about the third pull.
With everything is dealt now and the next two times.
With little children's prayer (Mat. 11:25), Bert

¤ All his life, brother Branham had lived in the state of Kentucky in the United States. There in the town of Jeffersonville had been his congregation and church. From 1947 on some of his sermons were recorded. Click on the sermon year and then click on the speaker (and the play button) to listen to it:
https://branham.org/en/MessageAudio
Or as written English texts. Click on the bookmark to see the list of sermons:
https://table.branham.org/#/en/main
¤ In December 1962, he had realized that he had to move to the state of Arizona, what he and his family did in January 1963. That is what he told about it in the sermon 'Is This The Sign Of The End, Sir? (62-1230E)'.
A few points I have mentioned below.
¤
#200 And I was at Tucson, Arizona, in the vision, for it made it so purpose that He didn't want me to fail to see where it was at. I was picking a sand burr off of me, from the desert. And I said, "Now, I know this is a vision, and I know that I'm at Tucson. And I know that them little birds there represent something." And they were watching eastward. And all of a sudden they taken a notion to fly, and away they went, eastward.
#201 And as soon as they left, a constellation of larger birds came. They looked like doves, sharp-pointed wings, kind of a gray color, little lighter color than what these first little messengers was. And they were coming eastward, swiftly.
#202 And no sooner than they got out of my sight, I turned again to look westward, and there it happened. There was a blast that actually shook the whole earth.
#203 Now, don't miss this. And you, on tape, be sure you get this right.

#204 First, a blast. And I thought it sounded like a sound barrier, ever what you call it when planes cross the sound, and the sound comes back to the earth. Just shook, like, roared, everything. Then, it could have been a—a—a great clap of thunder, and lightning, like; I didn't see the lightning. I just heard that great blast that went forth, that sounded like it was south, from me, towards Mexico.

#205 But, it shook the earth. And when it did, I was still looking westward. And way off into Eternity, I saw a constellation of something coming. It looked like that it might have been little dots. There could have been no less than five, and not more than seven. But, They were in the shape of a pyramid, like these messengers coming. And when it did, the Power of Almighty God lifted me up to meet Them.

#206 And I can see It. It's never left me. Eight days has gone, and I can't forget it, yet. I never had anything to bother me like that has. My family will tell you.

#207 I could see those Angels, those shaped-back wings, traveling faster than sound could travel. They come from Eternity, in a split, like a twinkling of an eye. Not enough to bat your eye, just a twinkle, They were there. I didn't have time to count. I didn't have time no more than just look. Mighty Ones, great, powerful Angels, snow white; wings set, and heads. And They were, "Whew-whew!" And when it did, I was caught up into this pyramid of constellations.

¤

#210 Well, then I turned again. I thought, "Lord God, what does this vision mean?" And I wondered.

#211 And then it come to me, (not a voice) just come to me. "Oh! That is the Angels of the Lord, coming to give me my new commission." And when I thought that, I raised up my hands, and I said, "O Lord Jesus, what will You have me do?" And the vision left me. For almost an hour, I couldn't feeled.

Seven Angels of Heaven (2): Seventh Seal

Shalom,
^ God has His Own Way and place to reveal things. Through faith, Abraham was ready to go to a foreign land and to live in a tent as a stranger (Heb. 11:8-10).
Prayer of them who believe that the Lord Jesus is the only Way to the Father (John 14:6, Rev. 3:20), Bert

¤ 040163 William Branham and his family moved to the city of Tucson, Arizona, on the western side of the United States. And two months later he visited his home church, in Jeffersonville, on the eastern side of the United States. It was also announced that there would be spoken about the 7 seals.

In the 'Seventh Seal' sermon, 63-0324E, he explained what had happened near Tucson:
7Seal#266 Remember the constellation, of the vision of the Angels, when I left here to go to Arizona? [Congregation says, "Amen."—Ed.] You remember What Time Is It, Sirs? (The tape/message/preaching as mentioned on the former page.) ["Amen."] You remember that? Notice, there was only one great burst of thunder, and seven Angels appeared. That right? ["Amen."] One burst of thunder, seven Angels appeared, [~ Rev. 6:1,] <And I saw the Lamb when he had opened the first seal, and I heard, as it was the voice of a thunder, and one of the four beasts said, Come (and see).>

#267 Notice, one thunder, Seven Messages that's been sealed up and cannot be revealed until the last day, of this age. See what I mean? [Congregation says, "Amen."—Ed.]

#268 Now, have you noticed the mysterious part of this week? That's what It is. That's what It's been. It's been not a human being, a—a man. It has been the Angels of the Lord. Notice.

#269 There is witnesses, of three, sitting in here, that a week ago, a little over a week ago, I was up, way back into the mountains, nearly to Mexico, with two brethren that's sitting here. Picking cocklebur, or sandburs, off of my trouser leg; and a blast went off, that almost, looked like, shook the mountains down. Now, that's right. I never told my brethren, but they noticed a difference.

#270 And He said to me, "Now be ready. Go east. Here is the interpretation of that vision." See? Now, to let you know, Brother Sothmann has not got the game that he went after. We was trying to get it for him. And He said, "Now, tonight, for a sign to you, he isn't going to do it. You must consecrate yourself at this time for the visitation of these Angels." And I felt beside myself, you remember.

#271 And I was in the west. The Angels was coming east. And as they come by, I was picked up with them, (you remember that?) coming east. [Congregation says, "Amen."—Ed.]

#272 And Brother Fred, in here tonight, is a witness, and Brother Norman.

¤

¤ And brother Branham told why everything in Heaven was silent. Or, to put it better, he spoke what he was allowed to say (cf. Rev. 8:1).

#299 …. "This will be the Third Pull, and you won't tell It to nobody." And in Sabino Canyon, He said, "This is the Third Pull."

#300 And there's three great things that goes with It. And one unfolded today, or, yesterday; the other one unfolded today; and there's one thing that I cannot interpret, because it's in an unknown language. But I stand right there and looked right straight at It. And this is the Third Pull coming up. [Brother Branham knocks on the pulpit three times—Ed.] And the Holy Spirit of God…Oh, my! That's the reason all Heaven was silent.

¤

#402 Because, before we even went into It, and I left to go west, the Lord showed me a vision one day, about ten o'clock, one morning. And I come and explained it here, that I had seen it; didn't know what it was. It was a constellation of seven Angels. We'll remember that. You'll get it on the tape, called, What Time Is It, Sir? Well, now, that is exactly what you're seeing now. The seven Angels…I was in the west.

#403 You remember, the little bitty messengers; they went east. The second messengers, the doves, little bit larger bird, they went east. And then I looked…They was with me, all the time. That was that First and Second Pull.

#404 Now, the Third came from the west, sweeping forward with great, terrific speed, and They picked me up. That was coming back east, with the mystery of these Seven Seals. Just like it said in—in Junior Jackson's dream, that the Lord let me interpret for him there, "On the inside of that pyramid, there was white Stone that wasn't written on." That's the reason I had to go west, to connect with these Angels' Message, to come back here to reveal It to the church. Remember, I said, "The next things that happen will be here at the church." That's just exactly.

#405 Another thing, I want you to notice what taken place. And if you're listening to the tape, of the What Time Is It, Sir?, you will notice that one Angel was very notable to me. The rest of them just was seemed ordinarily. But this Angel was a noted Angel. He was to my left, in the constellation in the form of a pyramid.

Seven Angels of Heaven (3): Impossible Explosion, Cloud, Etc.

Shalom,
^ William Marrion Branham would be one of the candidates to be the prophet Elijah sent by God in the end times of the churches. He loved to be in the wilderness like many prophets of the Old Testament. On his mother's side, he had a Native American Indian background. As a young child he learned to earn money by catching animals, because his family was the poorest of the poor. As a young husband he spent for his work a lot of time in the woods. And he has always been a hunter.

On the other hand, the leaders of many churches and of all kinds of spiritual groups have their ready judgments. For example, that Branham got lost at the end of his life and that it was never meant for him to become a teacher.

^ With the Internet you can find both harsh attacks on his words and incredible healing miracles in his ministry. Though all happened by 1965, when brother Branham died; back then there was not yet internet. Therefore, gradually personal testimonies are disappearing, because every year you have to pay to keep your internet pages up. And Google does not easily lead to such pages.

^ In my turn I have to say that it was only through brother Branham's teachings/preachings that I learned the contents of the Seals and the explanations of the entire Book Revelation. A better explanation cannot be found. Or if found, I would be interested to hear of it.

Prayer of them who think of themselves with sober judgment (Rm. 12:3), Bert

¤ In January 1963, brother Branham and his family had moved to the city of Tucson, Arizona.

February 28, 1963, shortly before sunset, a strikingly beautiful and mysterious cloud lingered in the northwest direction over Arizona. The cloud was at an impossibly high place where no clouds can appear, not to mention its special shape and its enormous size.

¤ About hundred photographs and two hundred reports were gathered of the cloud that bBranham later referred to. But around it has been a lot of uncertainty. In the beginning it took almost a month before it was reported on March 26, 1963 in the region's (Phoenix city) 'Arizona Republic' newspaper.

At that time, few people had a camera, let alone the painstaking development of the film into photographs. Among other things, that's why it had taken so long.

¤ Something was seemingly shown to the whole world, or more precisely to all interested people. God and his angels would be ready all the time. But, for example, the hunting season for javelina hogs from March 1-10 had not started. Therefore, bBranham's usual hunting in that area had not yet been possible. As well as there had been an important meeting 040363 more than 1000 miles away from the city of Tucson. Then from March 6-9 he was with two spiritual brothers northeast of Tucson hunting javelina hogs. Suddenly there was an impossible huge explosion. Of it there are many surprising details, see for example, https://www.williambranhamstorehouse.com/pdf_downloads/a%20high%20cloud%20and%20ring%20of%20mystery.pdf [Copy/type the whole link to your web browser and press 'Enter' to get the file visible]

¤ At the beginning of the document is said that Jesus Christ had more success through William Branham's ministry than through His Own. However, about such a remark bBranham himself had said that no greater works than Jesus did, can be done (e.g. 63-0627, #258, John 14:12).

Of the cloud is among others a picture shown and explained, which, turned to the right, shows the Face of the Lord Jesus, how the painter Hoffman had painted Him at the age of 33. BBranham had previously referred to this painting. Thus, one can get to know things what would otherwise be forgotten or dismissed as impossible events.

¤

¤ There are enough questions. Did the angels which he had previously seen in a vision and about whom he had spoken, belong to that cloud? It remains for each believer to ponder (5e and 5f§6(8)10).

One could notice divine miracles. Who could build in advance such an entity among many believers and the world? God's way of appearing to bBranham as angels would be in the context of the Book Revelation, where there is talked a lot about angels. In that way, the Lord Jesus could have been one of the seven angels (5d§6(8)10, Rev. 10:1-2).

¤

¤ In the 24th chapter of the Gospel by Matthew, Jesus Christ answered three questions of His disciples, of which the two last answers touched on our end-time {Mat. 24:3 (6h§6(8)10)}.

And two times He spoke of the coming of the Son of man and its sign in heaven, read Mat. 24:27 and 30.

¤ Belongs the picture of the cloud to the hunting incident is not hundred percent sure. Also because God hadn't wanted to make the cloud a public matter, according to bBranham. As regards the second answer, it means that every believer must alone solve this connection till the moment of Jesus' Presence, when in the air He will take ready believers up into Heaven {read 1c§1-3, Mat. 24:27(-28)}.

And as regards the third answer, as regards the sign of the consummation of our era, as regards the end of the sixth seal, the picture could be an additional answer {Mat. 24:30 (7e§67$_1$14)}.

~ ~ ~

B6 (Revelation §6,(8,)10, Seals Explained)

6h§6(8)10

First Seal

Shalom,

^ The Holy Spirit has had at least two main ways of revealing the secrets of the seals. That's what I noticed when I systematically analyzed, among other things, many of brother Branham's sermons.

In general, believers have focused on what bBranham had told about the secrets of the seals publicly and directly. That is how the warnings of the seals were spoken to the whole world. It was a comprehensive revelation [= S].

But without speaking of the seals, in every church age there had been revealed to believers in local groups one seal at a time in order to strengthen them. It was a near revelation [= s].

This time and from the explaining of the fifth seal on I also deal with the near revelation (6l§6(8)10, etc.).

Prayer of them who want to be patient until the Lord's 'Presence' (James 5:7-8, and 0c§Preface), Bert

¤ After discussing the background of the seals and the opening process, I now provide possible/impossible summaries of the explanations of the secrets of the seals. Though, it's impossible to sum it up in a few sentences. Brother Branham's sermon on each seal lasted over two hours. However, he said in the preaching of the sixth seal that the Lord Jesus had spoken of the same secrets of the six seals when He answered his disciples their end-time questions (63-0323, 6Seal Sermon, #136, etc.).

Jesus had first spoken about the temple buildings and said (Mat. 24:1-2), Mat. 24:2, <.... " ....Truly I tell you, not one stone here will be left on another; every one will be thrown down.">

¤ Later his disciples asked Him, Mat. 24:3 (=, 8e§89₁156), <"Tell us, when will these things happen, and what {will be} the sign of Your presence and of the consummation of the age/era?">

Before He gave these three answers, He first gave six summaries of the meanings of the seals, which follow one by one. Finally, 'Sixth Seal Explained' tells what will happen before the end of the consummation of the era. {In addition, too I refer to what I wrote at the beginning: 1c§1-3 (Mat. 24:4-14)}.

¤

¤ First, the symbol of the first seal, Rev. 6:1-2, <Then I watched as the Lamb opened one of the seven seals, and I heard one of the four living creatures say in a thunderous

voice, "Come!" 2. So I looked and saw a white horse, and its rider held a bow. And he was given a crown, and he rode out to overcome and conquer.>

The Lamb had been the only one worthy to receive and open the scroll sealed with seven seals (Rev. 5).

¤ When He had opened all the seals, He was seen as a strong Angel who came down from heaven and had a small opened scroll in his hand (5d§6(8)10, Rev. 10:1-2).

Each time God had spoken from His eternal Throne and announced the message of each seal, seven thunders. But when it was placed before John, they were sealed and presented as symbols. It cannot be revealed until the end time, as He said here (Rev. 10:3-7).

¤ The mighty rumble of thunder is the Voice of God. That's what the Bible says it is. People thought it was a thunder, but it was God. Jesus understood that (John 12:27-29).

Two thousand years ago, when the seal was opened in the form of a symbol, there was a rumble of thunder. Now in the end times, the thunder rolled as soon as the Lamb broke the seal. First it was God, next as a symbol, then it was revealed, three things. ¤

1S: This rider and white horse was the spirit and power of the Antichrist in the early churches! That's what bBranham told when the Holy Spirit had come and revealed that secret to him.

The Lord Jesus had warned about the same false anointed believers, Mat. 24:4-5, <Jesus answered, "See to it that no one deceives you. 5. For many will come in My name, claiming, 'I am the Christ,' and will deceive many. ...."

¤ But before the Slanderer/devil had sent his first service animal, God had already sent His first 'creature' against it. Four creatures near the Lamb, four powers for the believers. The first was like a lion (Rev. 4:7).

God had sent His Word and His Power, the Apostolic Teaching. Thus God confirmed His Word with Healings, Miracles, Visions and Power.

1s: Here my note. In about 90 AD the apostle John had warned believers about the same thing, 1John 2:18-19, <Children, it is the last hour; and just as you have heard that the antichrist is coming, so now many antichrists have appeared. This is how we know it is the last hour. 19. They went out from us, but they did not belong to us. For if they had belonged to us, they would have remained with us. But {their departure} made it clear that none of them belonged to us.>

In the first church age, during the Ephesian revival, the Holy Spirit had conveyed this secret to the true believers, a single clap of thunder. The revelation of the secret of the first seal repeats this warning.

Second Seal

Shalom,
^ With comprehensive explanations of the secrets of the seals is continued.
Prayer of them who seek God's Ways and Thoughts (cf. Isa. 55:9), Bert

¤ Summary of the secret of the second seal. First, its symbol, Rev. 6:3-4, <And when it [the Lamb] opened the second seal, I heard the second living creature say, "Come!" 4. Then another horse went forth. It was bright red, and its rider was granted permission to take away peace from the earth and to make men slay one another. And he was given a great sword.>
Again we are talking about the same rider, but his horse has changed. This is Satan again! But Satan in another form. This horrible treacherous spirit was incarnated. This spirit of doctrine was embodied in a man, and took the place of Christ. Then man had to be followed and worshipped instead of Christ.
¤ First, here follow all the revivals of the church ages. From 1960-12-04 till 1960-12-11 brother Branham had dealt with the first three chapters of the Book Revelation and had given a huge amount of details. It was a total of about 23 hours of preaching. From that his friend and fellow believer Lee Vayle prepared the book An Exposition Of The Seven Church Ages [An Exposition Of The Seven Church Ages], which (without a computer) was completed after Branham's car accident and death (1965-12). The revivals of the church ages (ChuRev) include the following successive time periods and star messengers (cf. 1ab§1-3):
1. The church age of Ephesus, 53–170.... AD, and the beginner of its revival, the apostle Paul.
2. The church age of Smyrna, 170–312.... . Here Irenaeus represented in the best way Paul.
3. The church age of Pergamum, 312–606...., with Martin (315-399).
4. The church age of Thyatira, 606–1520.... . The best example of an apostle was Columba.
5. The church age of Sardis, 1520–1750...., with Martin Luther (1483-1546).
6. The church age of Philadelphia, 1750-1906...., with John Wesley (1703-1791).
7. The church age of Laodicea, 1906-...., and the prophet 'Elijah' (Mal. 4:5-6).
¤
¤ Worldwide in the Christian society the fulfillment of the content of the second seal can be noticed. Archbishops and eventually popes were elected, who were more interested in worldly rulers than in God. Then the rider of the first seal dropped his bow, got off his white horse, and got on his red horse. Now he could kill anybody that didn't agree with him. It's the same man/system according to bBranham!

In the revival of the church of Pergamon 312 – 606.... in the Western and Eastern Roman Empire, the emperor Constantine (emperor years 306–337) was the first Christian emperor. In 325 he convened the Council of Nicaea. Regrettably, he also influenced the outcomes of the meeting and since that time the state and the church have been really married many times and in many ways.

¤ In 476 AD, the Western Roman Empire fell. Then it changed in the papal state. But the fornication of the church leaders of Rome with all kinds of political leaders just continued (cf. 4a§1317, Rev. 17:2).

When Satan had both the state and the church together, he formed his own religion. In that way he could do what he wanted to do. He had the power to kill anyone who disagreed with him. In those dark periods, political leaders were influenced to slaughter millions of true believers of God in every possible way.

¤ During the revivals ages of Pergamon and Thyatira, the spiritual power/violence of the Roman Catholic Church was annihilating. More and more it focused on one person, one church leader, the pope, whom the New Testament refers to as a false prophet (cf. Mat. 23:9; Rev. 16:13; 4e§1317, Rev. 19:20 and 20:10).

The spirit of the Antichrist in the universal Christian church continued in the church age of Thyatira. The darkness just tightened. The church of Christ could do nothing but work in love, faith and service, go from place to place, Rev. 2:18-19, <"To the angel of the church in Thyatira write: These are the words of the Son of God, whose eyes are like a blazing fire and whose feet are like polished bronze. 19. I know your deeds—your love, your faith, your service, your perseverance—and your latter deeds are greater than your first. ....">

¤ In God's plan, a creature that looked like a young bull had gone to fight against Satan's new system. A bull is a working animal. It was a church that did a lot of spiritual work. And the young bull is a sacrificial animal. Believers gave their lives as willingly as they could while Catholicism ruled the world for over a thousand years. They had to answer either yes or no. They had nothing against dying. If one had to die, it was okay. They went and died anyway. It was the spirit of that time (also 6h§6(8)10, Rev. 4:7).

The Lord Jesus had spoken about the second seal, Mat. 24:6, <".... You will hear of wars and rumors of wars, but see to it that you are not alarmed. These things must happen, but the end is still to come. ....">

Third Seal

Shalom,
^ The great features of the secret of the third seal came from brother Branham. The details of the history came from me, that is, through the 'human face'.
Prayer of them who always have reasons to be joyful (2Cor. 2:3; Rev. 19:7-9), Bert

¤ The Lamb opened the third seal, Rev. 6:5-6, <And when it [the Lamb] opened the third seal, I heard the third living creature say, "Come!" Then I looked and saw a black horse, and its rider held in his hand a pair of scales. 6. And I heard what sounded like a voice from among the four living creatures, saying, "A quart of wheat for a denarius, and three quarts of barley for a denarius, and do not harm the oil and wine.">
The rider of the first and second seals continued on a black horse. Again he changed his ministry.
¤ With the Reformation, the spiritual power of the Roman Church shrank. But not its political power. In addition to that, the Devil is the overall leader of the political world based on Jesus' words (4a§1317, Mat. 4:8-10).
With the powers of the nations, Satan continued to kill at a big scale many believers and people. Exactly in Europe, where the center of the popes of Rome was still.
¤ For a long time the world's most powerful weapons were invented in Europe and globally much property was destroyed. Also industry developed enormously, and globally the rich have become richer and the poor have become poorer. They are two examples how wheat and barley have become more expensive all the time.
But even as dark political rule intensified, the Truth of God's Word has really been revealed to Jesus' saints, who have been filled with the Oil of the Holy Spirit (e.g. Zec. 4:1-6).
¤ It has stimulated them everywhere. Wine tells about stimulation and excitement to rejoice and shout. Here the Lord Jesus had spoken 'in the midst of the four creatures'. The Revealing of God's Word has filled believers with joy and noise.
As Peter explained when the Holy Spirit was poured out for the first time, Ap.t. 2:15-17a, <".... These men are not drunk, as you suppose. It is {only} the third hour of the day! 16. No, this is what was spoken by the prophet Joel: 17. 'In the last days, God says, I will pour out My Spirit on all people. ....' "
¤
¤ The words of the third seal of the Lord Jesus had been, Mat. 24:7-8, <".... Nation will rise against nation, and kingdom against kingdom. There will be famines and earthquakes in various places. 8. All these are the beginning of birth pains. ....">
In Europe, nations have constantly risen against each other. There was constant competition particularly between the major powers, Great Britain, France, Germany and Russia. Then, with the First and Second World Wars, European power has collapsed.

Today, the EU as a fully pacifist force has tried to manage all the world's conflicts. It has been biased and anti-Christian, which has not solved but increased many problems. ¤ Earthquakes have been part of the world's birth pains throughout the ages. The Book Revelation speaks in several places of only one, the earthquake at the end of the world age (Rev. 11:13, 19; 16:18-19).

It will be a global and severe earthquake that is unparalleled (cf. Rev. 16:18-19).

¤

¤ The Blood of Jesus Christ had sent the Holy Spirit back to us, and the creatures of the first four seals helped guard the Holy Spirit in the churches.

The first had been like a lion, the second like a young bull. Now the one with a face like a man appeared (and at the end we see a creature that looks like an eagle in flight) (Rev. 4:7).

¤ There are four Gospels, four natures. The lion is the symbol of the tribe of Judah. Judah was the central and strongest tribe of the two tribes. It was the tribe that brought King David and Jesus Christ. It represented the Gospel according to Matthew. In the Gospel of Matthew, the God's Word was explained and confirmed the most of all with the texts of the Old Testament.

The spirit of the ox in the Gospel of Mark is seen in the fact that it is a gospel of deeds and works, which is more concise than words. It is the shortest of all the Gospels.

¤ The Gospel according to Luke is the only Gospel written by a pagan believer. Luke was a doctor. Human wisdom and human discernment are visible in this work. As well as in the Reformers and the believers of the following church age of Philadelphia. Under the leadership of many serious believers, both the world and faculties have been explored.

In the last gospel the apostle John published about 90 AD. the heritage of the early Christians and, of course, his own memories, which had not yet been published and which focused on miracles and deeper spiritual thoughts. There you can see the characteristics of the last creature, a flying Eagle. The eagle sees farther than all the other animals and represents especially prophets, and even God. Johannes focused on the invisible world. For example, he started with God and his Word, before the creation of the world (John 1:1-3).

Fourth Seal

Shalom,
^ The fourth seal speaks of strong final birth pains of the world, according to Jesus Christ's words. Likewise, during the period of the third seal there had been the beginning of the birth pains (6j§6(8)10, Mat. 24:8).
At the end of the birth pains, three different purified subjects are born {7th seal sermon (7d§67₁14)}.
But first, a group, born from above, is taken into Heaven.
Prayer of the called, the chosen, and the faithful ones for each and many others ones (Rev. 17:14b), Bert

¤ The Lamb opened that seal, Rev. 6:7-8, <And when it [the Lamb] opened the fourth seal, I heard the voice of the fourth living creature say, "Come!" 8. Then I looked and saw a pale green horse. Its rider's name was Death, and Hades followed close behind. And they were given authority over a fourth of the earth, to kill by sword, by famine, by plague, and by the beasts of the earth.>
In this horse have been mixed the colors and functions of the three first horses. The same Antichrist rider switches to a horse, that causes massive spiritual and physical death.
¤ From 1906, in the revivals of the church age of Laodicea, spiritual gifts had been found again on a large scale. But to spiritual gifts belong also duties. It is a must to test the spirits of the spiritual leaders, cf. 1John 4:1-3, <Beloved, do not believe every spirit, but test the spirits to see whether they are from God. For many false prophets have gone out into the world. 2. By this you will know the Spirit of God: Every spirit that confesses that Jesus Christ has come in the flesh is from God, 3. and every spirit that does not confess Jesus, is not from God. This is the {spirit} of the antichrist, which you have heard is coming and which is already in the world {at this time}.>
In the end, there are true anointed believers and many false anointed ones (cf. Mat. 24:24).
¤ God allows many persons to be deceived (2The. 2:9-12), Rev. 16:13-16, <And I saw three unclean spirits that looked like frogs {coming} out of the mouths of the dragon, the beast, and the false prophet. 14. These are demonic spirits that perform signs and go out to all the kings of the earth, to assemble them for battle on the great day of God the Almighty. 15. "Behold, I am coming like a thief. Blessed is the one who remains awake and clothed, so that he will not go naked and let his shame be exposed." 16. And (he/)they assembled the kings in the place that in Hebrew is called Armageddon.>
Frogs are backward-looking spirits. The dragon's frog represents Satan's antichrist spirit, which prepares the world to think like the future antichrist president of the USA, who

would emphasize all kinds of pagan Christian values (cf. 4b§1317, Rev. 13:11; and 4c§1317, Rev. 13:12).

¤ The (seven-headed) beast and its frog represent the political powers of the world. For example, because of its influence, it is difficult for states to accept Israel's existence and activities.

The influence of the false prophet's frog can be seen in the emphasis on Christian traditions and the desire of different churches to show that they are all one, as the early church was. The establishment of the World Council of Churches was one of the outcomes (cf. John 17:21 and 4c§1317, Rev. 13:14-15).

¤ In general, the anti-Christian spirit, which already affected the believers of the first church age, is taking over the end-time church (5a§6(8)10, Rev. 3:14-22, and 5b§6(8)10).

That is how the nature of the persecutions changes. It no longer happens among people, but has been transferred to the spirits' world. That is why God sends still a new power, his fourth 'creature', a flying eagle creature. With it's help the spiritual challenges of the end time can be approached successfully (6j§6(8)10, Rev. 4:7).

¤ We need the right answers to defend against Satan's powerful attacks. A prophet in the spirit of Elijah helps believers in the end time of the churches to prepare to meet their Lord and avoid the horrors of the Greater Tribulation {5b/5c§6(8)10, Mal. 4:(1-)6}. {And during the Greater Tribulation time, two prophets/witnesses will prepare the 144,000 (7abcde§67₁14).}

Thus, before the time of the Greater Tribulation, the Lord Jesus will come like a Thief and take His bride-believers born from above into Heaven (John 3:3; 3a§12, Gal. 4:24 and 26; 1The. 5:2 (3c§12, 1The. 4:15b-5:3)}.

¤

¤ After the rapture, there are no more obstacles for the Antichrist-man to take over the church. Led by Satan, as this one will be thrown out of Heaven at that time (3f§12, Rev. 12:13).

Then the president of the United States will open his heart for it as Judas Iscariot once did (3c§12, John 13:27a).

¤ Later, I explain the unforgivable mistake of the president {Deu. 29:16-21 (8d§89₁156)}.

At the same time the second beast in the 13th chapter of Revelation becomes the seventh head of the first beast.

¤ Over the course of two thousand years Rome (the sixth head) and many, including the Jewish people, have agreed and have together persecuted Jesus Christ and His followers. It has been an evil and strengthened covenant (3d§12, Dan. 9:27).

But the moment that the United States joins this covenant, the leaders of Israel find, that they must get out of it {Rev.13:12 (7b§67₁14)}.

Fifth Seal (+ seals 1,2,3,4)

Shalom,
^ The Seals are a package of secrets which has been revealed in at least two different ways. Until now, I have mainly dealt with the symbols of the seals as events of the entire Christian society, as events of the whole world, as I wrote before (6h§6(8)10).
But between the lines could be noticed that first the secret of one seal had been revealed in the local churches of that church age. In each revival age, the revealing of one seal at a time.
Prayer of them who want to bear fruit {Mat. 13:(1-)23}, Bert

1s: The first seal belonged to the revival of the first church age, the Ephesian church age, from 53 till at least 170 (6i§6(8)10, ChuRev).
During that time, the Holy Spirit had warned about the antichristian spirit in some Christians {cf. 6h§6(8)10, 1John 2:18-19}.
2s: In the revival of the second church age, of Smyrna, the years 170 – 312.... , local anti-Christian church leaders emerged according to the secret of the red horse of the second seal. False apostles who better got along with political leaders than with revival believers. They claimed to be believers, but in reality they were the synagogue of Satan (Rev. 2:9).
Many bloody persecutions followed, in which the true believers just sacrificed their lives (6i§6(8)10, 2S).
3s: In the revival of the church age of Pergamon 312 – 606.... in the Western and Eastern Roman Empire emperor Constantine (emperor years 306–337) was the first Christian emperor. However, he made good and still more wrong decisions (cf. 6i§6(8)10, emperor Constantine).
At the same time according to the revelation of the black horse many so called Christian political leaders emerged everywhere. They claimed to be believers, but in reality they represented the seat of Satan (Rev. 2:13).
4s: In the church age of Thyatira 606 – 1520.... the prophetess Jezebel and her teaching was a type of the Roman Catholic church. A woman is in the Bible e.g. a symbol of a church. The pope and his church had become more important than God's Word. It was the warning of the messenger of the fourth church. There was only death (Rev. 2:18-29).
In all these church ages Rome has been the central power, the sixth head of the first beast, the political leader of the world, first as political power, then as spiritual power (4a§1317).
¤
¤ Next, my summary of the fulfillment of the first four seals in universal Christendom:

1S (6h§6(8)10): In the Ephesian church age, Satan's anti-Christian spirit had influenced some of the ordinary believers to leave the churches. In the following church age in Smyrna, this spirit also influenced some of the church leaders. As a result all kinds of conflicts arose between the churches, and many churches separated from each other.

2S (6i§6(8)10): In the church ages of Pergamon and Thyatira, 312 – 1520.... , Satan's spirit was embodied in archbishops and popes. These interfered in politics and influenced which churches were called real churches and which kinds of churches should be banned.

3S (6j§6(8)10): In the church ages of Sardis and Philadelphia, 1520 – 1906.... , this spirit embodied itself in the political leaders of Europe, from what many wars followed. And worldwide, leaders of the Roman Catholic Church were led into adulterous relations with cults of all kinds of local idols.

4S (6k§6(8)10): In our Laodicean church age, many believers are anointed with the wrong spirit. It is a terrible spiritual tribulation. In addition, in the coming Greater tribulation time, this spirit will anoint the antichrist man to lead the Christian world.
¤

5s: In the fifth church age, in the Sardisean Revival, 1520 – 1750.... , the Holy Spirit had begun to speak of the secret of the fifth seal, Rev. 6:9-11, <And when it [the Lamb] opened the fifth seal, I saw under the altar the souls of those who had been slain for the word of God and for the testimony they had upheld. 10. And they cried out in a loud voice, "How long, O Lord, holy and true, until You avenge our blood and judge those who dwell upon the earth?" 11. Then each of them was given a white robe and told to rest a little while longer, until the full {number} of their fellow servants, their brothers, were killed, just as they had been killed.>

With the Reformation, also Jews came to faith everywhere, were filled with the Holy Ghost and began to study and to learn what had long been hidden under the Roman Catholic cover. At the same time, they came to understand what was said under the fifth seal to their murdered relatives. At one time these, that is, Israel, were hardened/blinded so that the Gentile believers would be saved (Rm. 11:25-29).

5S: Brother Branham said that the fifth seal applies to the orthodox Jews. They had their Law, 'Word of God', and they stuck to it. Therefore they died as martyrs. This fulfillment of the contents of the seal will continue until the end of the time of the Greater tribulation (3b§12/7d§67₁14, Zec. 13:6-9 and Mat. 26:31).

The same difficult future Jesus Christ had predicted for his Jewish followers, <Mat. 24:9-13, <".... Then they will deliver you over .... 13. But the one who perseveres to the end will be saved. ...."

"SEVENTH SEAL"

Shalom,

7S: In the year 1963 brother Branham had passed on comprehensive messages and teachings of the secrets of the Seals. In that way the symbols of six seals were explained fully and things of the Seventh Seal partly (cf. 5f§6(8)10).

7s: However, there is also a local message for the believers of the Laodicean church age, who have both heard and answered the knocking of the Lord Jesus (for example 5b§6(8)10, Rev. 3:20).

When Satan and its forces attack them, God has His countermeasures. He has wanted to reveal to them the core challenges and key opportunities of the spiritual war. This has always been the initial stage of the learning of the content of a seal. But in the case of the Seventh Seal, it is the final stage (cf. 6l§6(8)10).

Prayer of them who have a longing for Love and an answer of Love (1John 3:16), Bert

7S: It is necessary to squeeze out a few specialties of the last seal. Brother Branham had not been allowed to talk too much about this Seal, in the beginning.

Also he had said that the time for the seventh seal had not yet fully come (7Seal#323).

¤ The next day he had refused to disclose the remainder of it (7Seal#261-374).

Instead, bBranham had commented on that sermon, 7Seal#377-414.

¤ And he had accepted one sentence of the end of the remainder, 7Seal#415b.

After the death of bBranham, it was decided to publish all (cf. comments 7Seal#376 and 7Seal#415a).

¤

¤ Before all, bBranham and his family had to move to the town of Tucson in order to meet seven Angels in the air. In the vision two months earlier it had been said (cf. 7Seal#410).

Then it had happened, and he returned to speak of the secrets of the seals in his home church. Next the secrets of the seals were revealed one seal / one angel / one day at a time.

¤ In this way to every seal was belonging one angel of Heaven. However, the Angel of the Last Seal was different and very significant, he had said.

Thus it can be believed that this Angel was Jesus Christ Himself, as He appeared at the beginning of chapter 10 (5d§6(8)10, Rev. 10:1-2).

¤ But the moment when He would have fully appeared and the way He would finally appear, remained unclear. In that way it just has been written. Suddenly there is no more time. Just as there is no time in the Eternal God.

The Lord Jesus shouted, and seven thunders were heard. Two thousand years ago these messages of the seals were sealed and given as symbols. But in our end times they were revealed. And when the whole Word of God had been restored, it was said (Rev. 10:3-4), Rev. 10:5-7, <…. 'There should be time no longer.'….>

¤

¤ BBranham said that he had gone west for the blast (what had been God 'speaking). And he returned east with the Holy Spirit interpreting the unwritten Word (7Seal#319). The only unwritten Word in the New Testament was the moment of the Presence, the Becoming Present, of the Lord Jesus (Mat. 24:36).

¤ When God is there, everything is over. It silenced Heaven for about a half hour (Rev. 8:1).

Heaven was hushed by it. Not a thing there moved. The holy Cherubim and the Seraphim before God, saying, Holy, holy, holy, is the Lord God Almighty, were hushed! The angels quit singing! No praises. No altar service. Nothing! There was silence; hushed, deadly silence in Heaven, for a half hour.

¤ All the hosts of Heaven was awed by it, according to bBranham. They didn't know. There it was. They just stopped.

My comment: The Lord Jesus is the Secret and the Contents and the Fulfilment of the Seventh Seal. In addition, the opening of this Seal revealed the Secrets of all the seven seals. Not to mention the Contents of the Scroll.

¤

7s: Nowhere in the world has been a similar coincidence around the seven seals of Revelation. At the end all the image, text and time parts of the puzzle would dovetail both with each other and with the Bible, both with history and the future, both with the right and the wrong church, and so on.

After the revealing meetings of March 1963 came all the time more revelations. Till everything should have been said. The Perfect and Living Word of God of the end time should have become fully public.

¤ Surely with the Lord Jesus Christ, with the Perfect and Living Word of God, the believers in the end time will manage and prepare for the moment when He will appear face to face in the clouds in the air. Here as well as now He calls and is available: Rev. 3:20!

It's amazing that I've been allowed to write this page like this, 2021-08-07. It has been so significant that I understood for sure, that the Event of the Presence of the Lord Jesus in the clouds is less than a year away. Or again, it would be God's revelation that something special would happen by then (see 12c§1-22).

~ ~ ~

7a§67₁14

Learning and Fulfilling of the Seal

Shalom,
^ The sixth seal is dealt with using the chapters 6, 7, 11 and 14.
Prayer of them who in Christ are being built together with the Jewish people into a dwelling place for God in the Spirit (Eph. 2:22), Bert

5sS: Under the fifth seal, when the Reformation reorganized Europe, there were Jewish believers (Messianic Jews) who began to realize that God is using both fishermen and hunters to bring them and every other Jew back to their own land {Jer. 16:16 (8b§89₁156)}.
The opened secret of the souls under the altar reveals, that God has not forgotten His original chosen people. But, until the time period of the churches is over, the Jews will have to suffer blatant injustice of the nations. Then, they will return in two stages again into the center of God's caretaking.
6sS: During the Philadelphia revival, from 1750 to ~1906, understanding among (Messianic) believers increased. A terrible time of struggle for Jacob/Israel is coming (Jer. 30 and 31, cf. Gen. 32:24-32).
It is the Greater Tribulation time when the events of the sixth seal begin to be fulfilled. Then (the preaching of) the Gospel will return to a part of the Jewish people. It is the first stage, fulfilling the next answer of the Lord Jesus (6h§6(8)10, Mat. 24:1-14), Mat. 24:14, <".... And this gospel of the kingdom will be preached in all the world as a testimony to all nations, and then the end will come.">
7s: Next, He had directly spoken about the coming destruction of the temple (3e§12, Mat. 24:15-21).
And indirectly about the last half hour of time of the seventh seal (Mat. 24:21-28, also 6m§6(8)10).
¤ In this end time of the Gentile churches there would be an enormous spiritual tribulation {Mat. 24:21 (0b§Introduction)}.
But if you fly high enough, you will see spiritual food {1c§1-3 and 5g§6(8)10, Mat. 24:(27-)28}.
¤
6S: During the sixth seal nature turns completely upside down, Rev. 6:12-17, <And when I saw It [the Lamb] open the sixth seal, there was a great earthquake, and the sun became black like sackcloth of goat hair, and the whole moon turned blood red, 13. and the stars of the sky fell to the earth like unripe figs dropping from a tree shaken by a great wind. 14. The sky receded like a scroll being rolled up, and every mountain and

island was moved from its place. 15. Then the kings of the earth, the nobles, the commanders, the rich, the mighty, and every slave and free man hid in the caves and among the rocks of the mountains. 16. And they said to the mountains and the rocks, "Fall on us and hide us from the face of the One seated on the throne, and from the wrath of the Lamb. 17. For the great day of Their wrath has come, and who is able to withstand it?">

A terrible time is coming for the Jewish people and the whole world. Here is talked about similar plagues when the people of Israel left Egypt in the time of the Old Testament, according to brother Branham (63-0323, 6Seal Sermon). Of it the Lord Jesus had spoken in the verses: Mat. 24:29-31.

¤ Raise your head! The Rapture is the only Hope for the Gentile church members {Lk. 21:(25-)28(-33)}.

First, the Lord Jesus will cut His Harvest of Christians (3b§12, Mat. 24:32-44 and Lk. 21:29-33; and Rev. 14:14-16 (8e§89₁156).

¤ After that, the Spirit of God focuses solely on the people of Israel. It is the time of the Greater Tribulation and two witnesses will appear in the streets of Jerusalem and strike the world with all kinds of plagues, Rev. 11:5-6, <If anyone wants to harm them, fire proceeds from their mouths and devours their enemies. In this way, anyone who wants to harm them must be killed. 6. These witnesses have power to shut the sky so that no rain will fall during the days of their prophecy, and power to turn the waters into blood and to strike the earth with every kind of plague as often as they wish.>

The two Messianic witnesses are clothed according to the customs of the prophets of the Old Testament in sackcloth and powerfully they prophesy, Rev. 11:1-3, <Then I was given a {measuring} rod like a staff and was told, "Go and measure the temple of God and the altar, and count the number of worshipers there. 2. But exclude the courtyard outside the temple. Do not measure it, because it has been given over to the nations, and they will trample the holy city for 42 months. 3. And I will empower my two witnesses, and they will prophesy for 1,260 days, clothed in sackcloth.">

¤ The word temple speaks again of the inner room of the temple, God's place (on earth and in Heaven), which was spoken of in connection with the Antichrist, the Greek word 'naos' (4b§1317, 2 Thess. 2:3b-4).

In the Old Testament, it was called the Holy of Holies, which was inside the veil. The place on the other side of the veil was called the Holy. And in front of the veil stood the incense altar. With this altar, God e.g. shows that, led by those two witnesses, the prayers will reach Him (Exodus 26:31-34; 30:1-6).

¤ Around the Holy Place was the outer courtyard, with the burnt offering altar. In old times till there the people of Israel had been allowed to come and give sacrificial offerings to the sons of the priestly tribe of Levi to be presented to the LORD (Ex. 40:29-33; Ps. 96:8; cf. Ezek. 44:19; cf. Mal. 3:3-4).

From the text 'and they will trample the holy city for 42 months', we can understand that God's way of salvation is not yet open for the big majority of Israel's citizens. This is but the second stage {cf. Hep. 9:8 (9l§89₁156)}.

New Menorah Time of the Seal

Shalom,
^ The ages of the churches have represented one Menorah era (1a§1-3, Rev. 1:20).
Another Menorah era is the time of the Greater tribulation.
At the same time, we can notice a third Menorah era backwards.
Prayer of them who call upon the name of the LORD (Gen. 4:26), Bert

6S: We continue with the two witnesses who prophesied for 1260 days {7a§67₁14, Rev. 11:(1-)3}.
It is a new Menorah era, when they are compared to two olive trees (Rev. 11:1-6), Rev. 11:4, <These witnesses are the two olive trees and the two lampstands that stand before the Lord of the earth.>
¤ There is only one other place in the Bible that speaks of the menorah's two olive trees and two lampstands in the same way. The first exile of the Jewish people was just over. Some of the texts in question were already discussed (cf. 2b§45, Zec. 3 and 4), Zec. 4:1-4, <Then the angel who was speaking with me returned and woke me, as a man is awakened from his sleep. 2. "What do you see?" he asked. "I see a solid gold lampstand," I replied, "with a bowl at the top and seven lamps on it, with seven spouts to the lamps. 3. There are also two olive trees beside it, one on the right side of the bowl and the other on its left." 4. "What are these, my lord?" I asked the angel who was speaking with me.>
A new spiritual period had begun, in which the Holy Spirit worked with power (2b§45, Zec. 4:6), Zec. 4:11-14, <Then I asked the angel, "What are the two olive trees on the right and left of the lampstand?" 12. And I questioned him further, "What are the two olive branches beside the two gold pipes from which the golden oil pours?" 13. "Do you not know what these are?" he inquired. "No, my lord," I replied. 14. So he said, "These are the two anointed ones who are standing beside the Lord of all the earth.">
¤ The people had had two leaders. And the same plan God has for the Greater tribulation time. With the two witnesses, all the lights of the branches receive the Oil of the Holy Ghost and burn together. Firstly, it is the turn of the representatives of the original people of Israel to come to faith (3b§12, Rev. 12:1 and 14:1-5).
One hundred and forty-four thousand Israelites, 12,000 from 12 tribes, come to faith in 1,260 days. It is a tremendously powerful Revival compared to about 15,000-30,000 Messianic believers in Israel now (Rev. 7:4-8).
¤
¤ At the beginning of the time of Greater tribulation, Satan embodies in the president of the United States. As a result, the second beast of Rev. 13, the United States,

becomes the seventh head / world power of the first beast and an ally of Rome (6k§6(8)19, John 13:27a, and Rev. 12:13).

Then it begins to speak 'arrogant and blasphemous words' against God 1260 days (4b§1317, Rev. 13:5-6).

¤ For example, when it's Roman Catholic president starts to promote the pope's views, that the old city of Jerusalem does not belong to Israel (4c§1317, Rev. 13:12).

Thus, Israel is forced to break away from this covenant and a terrible tribulation begins {3e§12, Dan. 12:1(-3)}.

¤ At the same time, the two witnesses strongly criticize the president's claims and oppose any attempts to silence them. They also torment their opponents with all sorts of plagues. But in the end, the United States (and other nations of the world) will kill them (Rev. 11:1-10), Rev. 11:7, <When they [two witnesses] have finished their testimony, the beast that comes up from the Abyss will wage war with them, and will overpower and kill them.>

It is the Armageddon war of many nations against Israel and Jerusalem (6k§6(8)10, Rev. 16:(13-)16).

23W: Then the whole world wonders about the peace when it no longer hears or suffers new plagues from the mouths of the two witnesses. Television shows the bodies of the witnesses lying in the street. At the same time, the armies of the nations continue to exterminate the population of Jerusalem. But suddenly it happens (Rev. 11:8-10), Rev. 11:11-14, <But after the three and a half days, the breath of life from God entered the two witnesses, and they stood on their feet, and great fear fell upon those who saw them. 12. And the witnesses heard a loud voice from heaven saying, "Come up here." And they went up to heaven in a cloud as their enemies watched them. 13. And in that hour there was a great earthquake, and a tenth of the city collapsed. Seven thousand were killed in the quake, and the rest were terrified and gave glory to the God of heaven. 14. The second woe has passed. Behold, the third woe is coming shortly.>

After the coming to faith of the 144,000 and the ascending of the two witnesses to heaven, the rest of the Jewish people is amazed. And full-scale war is going on. Then Jerusalem and the whole earth rumbles.

¤ Suddenly it notices God's Hand! Seven thousand more died, but 'the rest were terrified and gave glory to the God of heaven'. Now it perceives that God is on their side against the heathen nations. The same earthquake on the Mount of Olives the prophet Zechariah had spoken about. The mountain where had been two Islamic mosques, has turned into a big valley. It had been prophesied in their Bible, their Tenach Holy Book. With their spiritual eyes, they see that their LORD is already standing there (Zec. 14:3-5 and 10-11).

Based on their history, the Jewish people knows that this LORD is Jesus Christ (Acts 1:11-12).

144,000 Israelites, and Three Woes

Shalom,
^ Last time and this time <u>and several other times I'm going to deal with the woe-cries. It's an in-depth study. Therefore, at the beginning of such paragraphs, they are indicated by the letters W and/or w.</u>
Prayer of them who seek God's workmanship/poem/handiwork for their own lives {Eph. 2:10 (3c§12)}, Bert

6S1W: In the time of the Greater tribulation, the nation of Israel is being prepared to come to faith as a whole. First, the Holy Spirit will fill only a part of the people of Israel. Through the two witnesses the 144,000 Israelis will receive Jesus Christ as their personal Savior.

These 144000 can be found in the Book Revelation, when you notice the signs of the times. The First World War / first woe ended in a very strange way. The peace treaty was signed on 11/11/1918 at 11 a.m. (cf. Mat. 16:3), Rev. 7:1-3, <After this I saw four angels/messengers standing at the four corners of the earth, holding back its four winds so that no wind would blow on land or sea or on any tree. 2. And I saw another angel/messenger ascending from the east, with the seal of the living God. And he called out in a loud voice to the four angels/messengers who had been given power to harm the land and the sea: 3. "Do not harm the land or sea or trees until we have sealed the foreheads of the servants of our God.">

¤ The New Testament talks about the eleventh-hour workers. They got the same salary as the ones who had been hired first. The 144,000 Israelites can be compared to them (cf. Mat. 20:9).

They had to be protected with a seal for their future spiritual work. 12,000 from twelve tribes (Rev. 7:4-8).

¤ They are God's 11th hour spiritual worker men/women. The first of them had just been born. And God knew who would still be born (cf. Rev. 13:8b).

For their sake He had commanded these angels to hold back the four winds of the world, as wind is the spiritual symbol of spiritual and physical warfare.

¤

¤ God has used world wars for his own purposes. And He does nothing without informing his prophets (cf. 5c§6(8)10, Amos 3:1-15).

Thus, we can learn that the creation is pregnant and is eagerly waiting for the revelation of the sons of God (Rm. 8:19-22).

5T1W: At the same time, God has announced that three woe-cry events are coming, Rev. 8:13, <And as I observed, I heard an eagle flying overhead, calling in a loud voice, "Woe! Woe! Woe to those who dwell on the earth, because of the trumpet blasts about to be sounded by the remaining three angels/messengers!">

The first woe belongs to the fifth trumpet {Rev. 9:12a (9j§89$_1$156); 9k§89$_1$156}.

67T23W: The second woe belongs to the sixth trumpet and the third to the seventh trumpet (cf. Rev. 11:14).

The trumpet angels are angels in heaven (5c§6(8)10, Rev. 8:2).

123w: In heaven the blowing of those trumpets is decided, but on earth three woe-messages have had to be preached. Already in 1954, brother Branham told in a veiled way that his message was fulfilling the third angel's message {(1. https://table.branham.org/#/en/main - 2. book mark – 3.:) 54-0513, #30-31}.

Based on that, I have connected the messengers/angels of Revelation 14 with the messengers who have been the messengers of the last three church ages. In that way, the leader of the revival of the church age of Sardis had to warn the people in his time in the following way (6i§6(8)10, ChuRev, since 1520 starting with Martin Luther), Rev. 14:6-7, <Then I saw another messenger/angel flying overhead, with the eternal gospel to proclaim to those who dwell on the earth—to every nation and tribe and tongue and people. 7. And he said in a loud voice, "Fear God and give Him glory, because the hour of His judgment has come. Worship the One who made the heavens and the earth and the sea and the springs of waters.">

¤ E.g. this message Martin Luther would have preached in continental Europe under the leadership of the Holy Spirit, in his time. But from God's point of view only a small part of the people had really come to faith in the revival of the Reformation (Rev. 3:1, 4). E.g. sanctification and spiritual deepening had been missing.

¤ And sins should not be forgiven through priests. It is done by water baptism in the name of Jesus Christ (Acts 2:38).

The First World War was the implementation and fulfillment of the first woe-cry.

¤

¤ Another woe-cry warning message belonged to the revival of the Philadelphian church age in Great Britain and its colonies (1b§1-3, Rev. 3:7-13; 6i§6(8)10, ChuRev, since 1750 starting with John Wesley), Rev. 14:8, <"Fallen, fallen is Babylon the great, who has made all the nations drink the wine of the fury of her fornication.">

At the same time as the need for sanctification was preached, one should warn about the hopeless situation of continental Europe, where Babylon the Great, the Rome of the popes, had continued to exert political influence. Later in World War II, Western Europe weakened fatally as predicted. In both world wars, the losses in the number of soldiers were enormous {4a§1317, the mystery of mother prostitute Babylon the Great (Rev. 17:5, 7)}.

All Jews Come to Faith

Shalom,
∧ Next is continued with the third woe-cry.
Prayer of them who believe that we may live under the Grace of the Lord Jesus (e.g. 1Cor. 16:23), Bert

6S3w: Preaching (and explaining) against among others the mark of the beast brother Branham had done a lot and many times, for example since 1954 (7c§67₁14, 54-0513), Rev. 14:9-13, <And a third messenger/angel followed them, calling out in a loud voice, "If anyone worships the beast and its image, and receives its mark on his forehead or on his hand, 10. he too will drink the wine of God's (holy-) fury, poured undiluted into the cup of His (full-grown-) wrath. And he will be tormented in fire and sulfur in the presence of the holy angels and of the Lamb. 11. And the smoke of their torment rises forever and ever. Day and night there is no rest for those who worship the beast and its image, or for anyone who receives the mark of its name." 12. Here is a call for the perseverance of the saints who keep the commandments of God and the faith of Jesus. 13. And I heard a voice from heaven telling me to write, "Blessed {are} the dead—those who die in the Lord from this moment on." "Yes," says the Spirit, "they will rest from their labors, for their deeds will follow them.">

All this will be fulfilled during the Greater tribulation time according to the sixth seal. The message and purpose of this seal is purification, the purification of the sleeping virgins, of the people of Israel, and of the earth (7Seal#387-390).

123W: The world has already experienced two world war woe-cries. But everyone who has watched the world situation of today, knows in his/her heart, that the third one is coming and will be terrible.

However, after the Third World War, i.e. the last great waves of contractions of the third woe-cry, at the end of the Greater tribulation time, the babies are born. As it has been foretold (3e§12, =), Isa. 66:8, <Who has heard such as this? who has seen anything like these? Can earth / a land be made to bring forth in one day? shall a nation be born at once? For as soon as she travailed, Zion also has borne her sons.>

¤ First, the 144,000 notice the wounds on their Messiah's, Jesus Christ's, chest (Zec. 13:6).

After accepting Him in faith as Saviour and Leader of their lives, they go all over the world to evangelize. They are messianic Israelis, who keep 'the commandments of God' and hold to 'the faith of Jesus' and who are terribly persecuted (also 3f§12, Rev. 12:12b---17).

¤ When during the Greater tribulation time the mark of the beast appears, the 144,000 will preach with both their actions and words that one must not worship the beast or its image, and must not take the mark on one's forehead or hand, because later in front of God's judgment throne one will end up directly into the lake of fire (cf. Rev. 20:11-15).

They are the firstfruit of the people of Israel (Rev. 14:4c).

¤ Verse Zec. 13:7 Jesus had referred to, when He was taken prisoner (Mat. 26:31).

Next, Zechariah had predicted that two-thirds of the Jewish people will be cut off and perish, but a third part will be left {3b§12, Zec. 13:(6-)8(-9)}.

¤ For two thousand years it has been refined and tested like silver and gold (Zec. 13:9a). In the end, the remaining third part would stand against an impossibly large superiority. In that moment, as a whole people, it cries out Jesus' name for help. And He answers and says to it, Zec. 13:9c, < 'It {is} My people,' and it says, 'The LORD {is} my God.'">
¤

¤ God uses the conflict between the Jews and the Palestinians around the city of Jerusalem as a cup of drunkenness to all nations. Therefore, at the end of the Greater tribulation time period, the vast majority of them will be involved in besieging Jerusalem and Israel (Zec. 12:1-3 and especially 2).

Jerusalem will be captured, Zec. 14:1-2a, <Behold, a day of the LORD is coming when your plunder will be divided in your presence. 2. For I will gather all the nations for battle against Jerusalem, and the city will be captured, the houses looted, and the women ravished. Half of the city will go into exile,>

¤ Israel's like-minded states are also involved in the attack, until the Third World War / third woe-cry suddenly breaks out and they are destroyed {9l§89₁156 (Zec. 14:1-2a)}.

At that moment for the people of Israel every hope is lost. Thus, as a whole nation, it is ready to cry out to God. One after another is baptized by the fire baptism of the Holy Spirit, and at the same time the earth is purified by the fire of atomic bombs (Mat. 3:11b-12).

¤ Until Jesus answers, and His people answers to Him. After that Zechariah's text continues, Zec. 14:2b-4a, <but the rest of the people will not be removed from the city. 3. Then the LORD will go out to fight against those nations, as He fights in the day of battle. 4. On that day His feet will stand on the Mount of Olives, east of Jerusalem,>

On a white horse, the Lord Jesus Christ with the armies of heaven will appear. The beast and the false prophet are thrown alive into the lake of fire and the other attackers are killed (Rev. 19:11-21).

¤ Next, in His thousand-year Kingdom, the Lord Jesus will reign with His Bride people (2c§45, Rev. 20:4-6, and 3b§12, 1Pet. 2:9-10).

However, all nations will be ruled with an iron scepter (Zec. 14:16-19 and Rev. 12:5).

The Word Hour in the Book of Revelation

Shalom,
^ In Revelation, the word hour has not always been translated by the same word hour, even if it was not difficult.
Prayer of them who wash their robes (Rev. 22:14), Bert

¤ From God's point of view, one hour can be over in one day or in a moment or in many years, as the apostle Peter explained (2Pet. 3:8).
Likewise, the length of an hour can be different, but the basic meaning of an hour is that it refers to some span of time.
7Ss7T: An unusually important event silenced Heaven for `about half an hour´(6m§6(8)10, Rev. 8:1).
Another extremely important event ends the half-hour silence of the seventh Seal, when the seventh trumpet is blown in Heaven: the rapture (5d§6(8)10, Rev. 7:1-8, etc.).
6S: After that, the end time scenario is predicted with the accuracy of a day. The next Greater tribulation time will last 1335 (=1260+30+45) days (3e§12, Dan. 12:11-12/13). Next, Christ's thousand-year's Kingdom will be started and experienced (Rev. 20:1-6).
¤
23W: Or in more detail, after 1260+3.5 days {7b§67₁14, Rev. 11:3, 11-14}, Rev. 11:13-14, <And in that hour there was a great earthquake, and a tenth of the city collapsed. Seven thousand were killed in the quake, and the rest were terrified and gave glory to the God of heaven. 14. The second woe has passed. Behold, the third woe is coming shortly.>
This word hour refers to the time period of 30 days, as only two periods remain.
6Ss: During the Greater tribulation time period the sixth seal will get its fulfillment. There are investigative judgments for left behind believers of the Gentiles and the people of Israel. A great earthquake is mentioned at the beginning {7a§67₁14, Rev. 6:12a(-17)}.
As BBranham had emphasized. An earthquake occurred on Good Friday when Christ was rejected (Mat. 27:51-53).
And He was rejected again in the Laodicean church age (Rev. 3:20 and 8:5).
¤ Plus a second quake is mentioned, above. Between the quakes, the lights of the sun, moon and stars will be shaken in many ways. Here they can be seen as the spiritual symbols of the nation of Israel, as I explain under the fourth trumpet {Gen. 37:9-10 (cf. 9i§89₁156)}, Rev. 6:12b-17, <…. and the sun became black like sackcloth {made} of hair, and the full moon turned blood red, 13. and the stars of the sky/heaven fell to the earth ….>
During the Greater tribulation time, the 144,000 Israelites will be terribly persecuted around the world, and at the end of it many nations will attack and capture Jerusalem.

There is very little gospel light and hope left in Israel (7d§67₁14, Zec. 12:1-3; 14:1-2a), Zec. 14:6-7, <On that day there will be no light, the luminaries will die out. 7. It will be a day known only to the LORD, without day or night; but when evening comes, there will be light.

67T23W: After the second earthquake the second woe-cry, the sixth trumpet, `has passed´, has ended. Plus, after the 30 days period begins the Third World War/woe-cry, which belongs to the seventh trumpet {third woe, Rev. 11:14b-19 (8a§89₁156)}.

It is the next 45-days period, which is under the smoke of all kinds of destruction weapons 'without day or night'. But at the end of this month and a half, which refers to the full moon of the next month in the middle of the month, 'there will be light'. {At the same time traces of atomic bombs, the rotting of the flesh of Israel's enemies, are seen (Zec. 14:12)}.

¤ Everywhere in the world the sign of the Son of Man will ignite the sky as the sign of the consummation of the era of the Gentiles {Mat. 24:30, and 5g§6(8)10, Mat. 24:3; Rev. 1:7. (And generally Rev. 6:14-17 and 19:11-21)}.

Simultaneously the Jewish nation is successful and consumes all the surrounding nations (Zec. 12:4–13:5; 14:13-15).

And during the next thousand years, the waters of the gospel will flow to Jews and Gentiles (Zec. 14:8-9).

¤

¤ Here are all the other texts in the Book of Revelation where the word hour is used:

Rev. 3:3b, <If you do not wake up, I will come like a thief, and you will not know the hour when I will come ….>

Rev. 3:10, <Because you have kept My command to persevere, I will also keep you from the hour of testing that is about to come upon the whole world, to test those who dwell on the earth.>

Rev. 9:15, <…. angels who had been prepared for this hour and day and month and year were released>

Rev. 14:7a, <…. "Fear God and give Him glory, because the hour of His judgment has come. ….">

Rev. 14:15b, <"Swing Your sickle and reap, because the hour has come to harvest; for the crop of the earth is ripe.">

As well as the following places where the word 'one' is used in addition to it:

Rev. 17:12, <The ten horns you saw are ten kings who have not yet received a kingdom, but will receive one hour of authority as kings, along with the beast.>

Rev. 18:10, <…. "Woe, woe to the great city, the mighty city of Babylon! For in one hour your judgment ….">

Rev. 18:16-17a, <…. "Woe, woe to the great city, …. 17. For in one hour such fabulous wealth has been destroyed!"

Rev. 18:19, <…. "Woe, woe to the great city, …. For in one hour she has been destroyed.">

~ ~ ~ ~ ~ ~

Seven Trumpets in Heaven

Shalom,
^ The plagues of the bowls belong to the judgments of the Trumpets, Book of Revelation chapters 8, 9, 11, 15 and 16.
However, explaining the secrets of the Trumpets would not be self-evident....
With prayer of the living letters of Christ (cf. 2Cor. 3:3), Bert

1-7T: When brother Branham had tried to rent a large meeting place, where he could preach to many people as regards the seven trumpets, everything failed. In the end, it was only possible to arrange a regular meeting. The reason he mentioned was that God forbade him from talking of the trumpets. The trumpets belong to the Jewish people, God had answered when he had asked for an answer. Thus, the topic and content of his sermon changed to the topic of 'The Feast of the Trumpets', from which also the explanation is found (64-0719M).

In the book Revelation, you find seven angels in heaven with trumpets, and seven star messengers of the churches on earth, who are trumpet blowers on earth. During bBranham's life, e.g. the secrets of the seals were revealed, as if he had been the messenger of the seventh church, the church of Laodicea (5c§6(8)10, =), Rev. 10:7, <".... But in the days of the voice of the seventh messenger/angel, when he is about to sound his trumpet, the mystery of God will be fulfilled, just as He evangelized to His servants the prophets.">

¤ Based on the message of this text, it can be believed that he was allowed to convey all the truths that God had wanted to reveal to us believers of the Laodicea revival. At the same time, with his trumpet he declared a spiritual war against all the forces of darkness (5c§6(8)10, 1Cor. 14:8-9).

The seventh trumpet of heaven instead initiates the Rapture of believers (cf. 5d§6(8)10, Rev. 11:15-19).

¤ Simultaneously it ends the age of the Laodicean church and starts the Greater tribulation time, at the end of which the whole earth will burn as an oven (1d§1-3, Mal. 4:1-6).

Similarly, the other trumpets would represent similar periods of judgments (Rev. 8:5).

¤

1-7S6T: A lot of background information was given by bBranham in the Feast of the Trumpets sermon. For example, the revelation of the secrets of the seven seals takes place during the period of the sixth trumpet. Just as in the book Revelation, after the symbol of the sixth trumpet, seven thunders are mentioned (Rev. 9:13–10:4).

The sixth trumpet was blown when the revival of the sixth church, the Philadelphian church age, had completely died out. At some point after 1906 (cf. 6i§6(8)10, ChuRev). ¤ During the period of the sixth trumpet judgment, the Lord Jesus Christ appeared in 1963 as a mighty Angel between Heaven and earth, and in his Hands was a small opened Scroll (6h§6(8)10, Rev. 10:1-3-7).

All seven seals of the Scroll had been opened and the secrets of six seals were revealed through Brother Branham. But the Secret of the Seventh Seal remained partially unrevealed. It was the Appearance of the Lord Jesus Christ on earth (6m§6(8)10).

7S: Brother Branham did not tell when the Appearance of the Lord Jesus, i.e. the revelation of the entire Word with all its truths, was fulfilled.

However, it should have been before his death, 12.1965.

¤

1-7S1-7T: When it is believed that the (last four) trumpets and their explanations belong to the people of Israel, the order of the Book Revelation begins to live and to become understandable. We see that the entire package of the first six trumpets and the seventh trumpet are mentioned separately (Rev. 8:2–9:21 and 11:15–19).

As well as the Seals (Rev. 6 and 8:1).

6S6T: The revelation of the secrets of the seals therefore took place during the sixth trumpet judgment. Likewise, according to bBranham, the revelation of the contents of the trumpets must take place during the investigative judgment of the sixth seal (7a§67₁14, Rev. 6:12-17).

During the Greater tribulation time of the sixth seal, the two witnesses will strike the world with all kinds of plagues (7a§67₁14, Rev. 11:5-6).

1-6T: And the 144,000 will come to faith through their spiritual work (7b§67₁14, Rev. 11:4).

At the same time, the witnesses reveal to the 144,000 Israelites the secrets of the first six trumpets.

7S: The Rapture has taken place and the half-hour period of the Seventh Seal has ended (Rev. 8:1).

The Secret Content of the Seventh Seal has been fulfilled and somehow revealed.

6T2W: Next, all kinds of signs of the six trumpets are written (Rev. 8:2–9:21).

But there is a major problem with revealing (the sixth trumpet and) the seventh trumpet. It is only after the great earthquake at the end of the Greater tribulation time that the second woe of the sixth trumpet is said to have passed {7b§67₁14, Rev. 11:(11-)14a(-14)}.

7T3W: After that will be seen the third woe-cry and the signs of the last trumpet (Rev. 11:14b-19).

The question is: will the time of the Greater tribulation last 7 years as commonly taught, or only 3.5 years? Though in the end, God Himself decides and the whole world will notice it (cf. 7d§67₁14, Zec. 14:2b-4a).

Plan of the Trumpets (and the Seals)

Shalom,
^ In Heaven is the Tabernacle, which was a pattern for the tabernacle on earth (Heb. 8:(1-)5).
Two thousand years ago Jesus Christ was slaughtered as the Lamb of God, as it had been planned (Rev. 13:8b).
After that, He, our High Priest of the Tabernacle in Heaven, ascended to God (Heb. 9:11-15).
Prayer of them who are humble and broken before God and tremble before his Word (cf. Isa. 66:1-2), Bert

¤ Forty days after Jesus Christ had risen from the grave He rose to God. And at the fiftieth day the Feast of Pentecost had been fulfilled with the coming of the Holy Spirit. God's Spirit had arrived in the church age to stay with and within the believers (John 14:17).
In his sermon on the Feast of Trumpets, brother Branham compared this 50 days' Atonement of Pentecost to the 50 years' Jubilee Atonement. First there had been 7*7 year-weeks (at the end of each one one trumpet of freedom had sounded), and the fiftieth year had been a joyful sounding of all the trumpets. This is how it had been taught and given as a commandment to the people of Israel (cf. Lev. 25).
¤ The same Atonement with God now awaits the Jewish people at the 50th spiritual year.
Therefore, the trumpets belong to the Jewish people, as God had said (8a§89₁156, Feast of Trumpets).
¤ Here you can see that at the end of each church age, in Heaven into one trumpet has been blown. And in the last Jubilee year-day, the Greater tribulation time, is the Feast of Trumpets. Into all trumpets is blown. Then 144,000 Israelis must be in Palestine/Israel. That's why God had to harden pharaoh's heart to drive them out of Egypt. And He had hardened Stalin, Mussolini, and done all that, to get them back to the promised land (7a§67₁14, Jer. 16:14-16).
Before was discussed, that also one seal belongs to each church age (6l§6(8)10).
¤
¤ Seven church ages are seven different revivals, seven lampstands together with seven star-messengers (1ab§1-3, Rev. 1:20).
Every believer in the churches is called to be a Light together with the star-messenger (Mat. 5:14-16).

¤ Two thousand years ago, all lamp branches burned and gave Light. The light comes from God's Holy Spirit, as it is seen in Heaven. Before the throne of God seven different Spirits, seven different Lights, are seen (2b§45, Rev. 4:5b).

The first church age was almost perfect. Everything was there, the perfect Word with perfect teaching and perfect fulfillment. Men and women dressed like Christians. They prayed all night. And they were not ashamed of the manifestations of the Spirit.

¤ But gradually among the believers Love cooled and Faith was abandoned. In the fallen world there are all kinds of attacks.

Believers started to organize the movement and directed it with human power. One led and the others had to be quiet. The influence and freedom of the Spirit went. The shout of joy disappeared. In this way, they kept the shape, but the fire was gone and the blackness of the ashes was almost all that was left. Churches and separated churches had appeared around God's Message. It's a man's doing. They are hustle clubs.

¤ When everywhere the revivals of that church age had gone out, one trumpet was blown in Heaven. That ended that age. The lampstand of that church was removed (Rev. 2:5).

It executed God's temporary trumpet judgment on those believers who did not continue in the spirit of revival and being led by the Holy Spirit.

¤ Six other Lights were left. Some of the believers had not failed to act. Fiery prayers had already led them forward. Constantly they had sought the revelation of the Holy Spirit, and the Word of God, and the living Word. Thus the Power of the Holy Spirit had been found again.

In this situation a new plan had been needed. God had wanted to tell what the new spiritual problems were about. That's how the Holy Spirit came along in the counterattack.

1-7s: In each church age, one seal was opened. First, it was announced in Heaven and opened. One secret God revealed. Next, the star messenger caught it, though not fully yet revealed. In faith he had to go and proclaim that Message to the people. It started a spiritual war (63-0318, 1Seal, #63-64).

The Holy Spirit continued to confirm that Message. Resistance weakened. Finally, the contents of one of the seals had come up fully. By the way, the fifth, sixth and seventh seals prepare e.g. the coming revival in Israel and are about to be fulfilled. When in the seventh trumpet is blown, the Silence and Secrecy of the Seventh Seal ends, and the Great Tribulation begins with all kinds of plagues and wonders.

¤

1-7T: Similarly, the first three judgments of the heavenly trumpets tended to wake up sleeping Christians.

And the last trumpets have been spiritual wars for the Jewish people, with which it has been prepared to come to faith.

"TRUMPETS ARE OPENING"

Shalom,
^ I begin to deal with the symbols of the trumpets, what I had done for the first time 2021-06-06. By that time I had looked more closely at the plagues of the bowels, and suddenly a possible overall picture had begun to emerge.
I prayed for it and received the answer that dealing with the symbols of the trumpets (and the bowels) was no longer a forbidden subject, as it had been during brother Branham's time (8a§89₁156, Feast of the Trumpets).
^ It meant that the Presence of the Lord Jesus in the clouds and the returning of the Jewish people to God had come extremely near (also 6m§6(8)10, the Seventh Seal)!
Very soon the Meeting of the Lord Jesus in the clouds should take place. Are you ready for that?
^ God takes seriously all people who use His Name. On this base believers and parts of Revelation can be divided. The messages addressed to the churches and an understanding of the secrets of the seals are for real believers. For lazy believers and the future people of Israel are the judgments of the trumpets. The bowels are plagues to name Christians, e.g. to the astray gone anointed Christians, as well as to the whole world.
Trumpets and bowels both represent God's judgments.
In that way can be understood and believed, that one trumpet and one bowel will be executed at the same time (cf. Rev. 8:5 and 15:7-8).
Prayer of them who "stand on the sea of glass" and worship only God (cf. Rev. 15:2-4), Bert
[= "Holy and unblemished believers before God reflect Him as He is {Eph. 1:4(-14); Rev. 4:6},
submitted to the other believers and completely cleansed by the water washing of God's Word (Eph. 5:21-26)."]

7T: When the half-hour silence of the Seventh Seal ends, the symbols of the trumpets in Heaven begin to appear (8a§89₁156, Rev. 8:2-9:21 ja 11:15-19).
The seventh heavenly trumpet has been blown and the Greater tribulation time begins.
¤ At the same time the believers of the Rapture will appear before the Throne of God (Rev. 7:9-17).
The Laodicean church age is completely over. At the end of it the Holy Spirit had already for a longer period no more functionated properly in the Christians of the Gentile nations (5b§6(8)10, Rev. 3:20).

¤ The Lord's acceptable year for the last two thousand years is totally over {Isa. 61:2a (8e§89₁156)}.

Serious judgments of God await humanity and all those believers who were not ready for the Rapture. As well as all who worship the beast and its image, and take its sign on their foreheads or in their hands. The last ones will later before God's Judgment Seat be sent straight to hell (Rev. 14:9-13 and 20:11-15).

¤ Just as God has different kind of judgments (cf. Mrk. 12:38-40).

And different kind of rewards (cf. 1Cor. 3:11-15).

¤

¤ Fully accepting of the gospel will further only happen among the people of Israel through the two witnesses (7b§67₁14, Rev. 11:4).

Such a severe physical persecution is coming for all mankind, what the believers had voluntarily suffered as regards of all kinds of great tribulation persecutions (0b§Introduction, Rev. 7:14).

¤ Also during their lives had existed signs and images of the beast (cf. Rev. 20:4).

With the beast having seven heads, God has described seven superpowers, which since the beginning of creation have succeeded in ruling over the whole known world {4a§1317 (Rev. 13 and 17)}.

¤

¤ In the past people were also marked. For example, in the time of the Old Testament God did not want the Israelites to use their own citizens as slaves. Every seventh year was a year of rejoicing, in which freedom was to be proclaimed to those own people slaves (Ex. 21:1-4).

But if any man did not want to depart, but was content with his slave master, then he was brought into the Temple, and his ear was pierced. It was a sign that he could never get free again. He had to serve his master for the rest of his life (Ex. 21:5-6).

¤ When someone rejects the Lord Jesus Christ as Saviour, Satan will mark him by his ear. He makes him so deaf that he is no longer able to hear the Truth.

Although he has ears, he can no longer hear (e.g. Rev. 3:22).

¤ When one hears the leaders of the world more than God, it means that he worships that beast and becomes a slave to Satan (cf. Rev. 13:8).

But he who wants to hear God and do His will, even if it costs his life, will finally meet God (Rev. 13:9-10).

¤ Also images of the beast had been created. That is personal cults or religions by which people were even more completely ruled. For example, king Nebuchadnezzar forced all his subjects to worship his statue (Dan. 3:1-7).

The Seal of God is the Baptism of the Holy Ghost, that you are sealed away in the Kingdom of God. And the mark of the beast is to deny It. Just as with the Jews then, with us Christians is sin like never before. And God looks for men/women, who sigh and groan over all the abominations committed here (Ezek. 9:1-6; Eph. 4:30).

Coming Economic Collapse

Shalom,
^ Seeing the coming economic collapse of the world is part of interpreting the signs of the times (Mat. 16:2-4).
Prayer of them who desire to listen to God rather than to men (Acts 4:19), Bert

¤ In almost all Western countries, debts of all kinds are rising faster and faster from year to year. Soon there will come the moment when moneylenders will no longer trust the ability of a state to pay back and neighboring countries will no longer be willing to help lend it their own money. As a result there is no more money to support the country's governmental systems and to buy the country's needs. That is how all living and all doing of work will come to nothing.

When the economy no longer functions, many debts remain unpaid. Next, in it's neighboring countries, it is noticed that their economies weaken strongly and begin to collapse.

¤ Global economic collapse is no longer just speculation in our time. Especially since economic development and God's signs match so well with each other. The time is coming when no one can buy or sell unless he has the mark of the beast (4d§1317, Rev. 13:16-18).

There I already dealt with the US debt.

¤ Among others with help of the following list, can be noticed that, in addition to many other countries, the EU's economy is weak and unstable, https://tradingeconomics.com/country-list/government-debt-to-gdp

The EU's debt was at the end of 2022 / 2021 / 2020 / 2019: 84,0 / 88,1 / 90.7 / 77,5 percent of gross domestic product.

¤ The economies of Western countries depend so much on each other that also an economic collapse starting here could be a possible cause for the bringing down of the American economy. However, its dollar is the main intermediary currency in world trade. With that, the economies of all countries in the world will come to a standstill or suffer. Then frantically will be looked for solutions.

Suddenly, a debt payer appears, what God had announced two thousand years ago. The name of the beast or the number of the name of the beast, a human being, the deputy of the Son of God, the pope (4d§1317, Rev. 13:17-18).

3w: However, there are always requirements for paying off a debt. What would they be? A reference to these can be found in the message of the third woe-cry (7d§67₁14, =), Rev. 14:9-13, <And a third messenger/angel followed them, calling out in a loud voice, "If anyone worships the beast and its image, and receives its mark on his forehead or on his hand, 10. he too will drink the wine of God's fury, poured undiluted into the cup of His wrath. And he will be tormented in fire and sulfur in the presence of

the holy angels and of the Lamb. 11. And the smoke of their torment rises forever and ever. Day and night there is no rest for those who worship the beast and its image, or for anyone who receives the mark of its name. ….">

Three things are mentioned at the same time. Worshiping the beast and its image and receiving the mark of the beast.

¤

¤ When the true believers are taken up into Heaven, the time of the Greater tribulation begins. The pope and the Roman Catholic Church are still for a while representing the seven-headed beast (4abc§1317, Rev. 13:3a).

This sixth head will rule the world until the president of the second beast, the president of the USA, opens his heart to Satan, who will be cast out of heaven before the Rapture (3f§12 and 6k§6(8)10, Rev. 12:13).

¤ Next, for some reason the value of the dollar will collapse (cf. 4d§1317, Rev. 13:16-18).

The emergency is great. The leading commercial role of the United States in the world and the global world trade are threatened. But suddenly, for example in the following manner, the president of the USA steps in front of his people with a few representatives of the World Council of Churches (=WCC), and starts speaking: "We were facing a huge challenge. But I just got a phone call. The Pope called and said that his Roman Catholic Church has a solution and I listened. Then I contacted the representative of the churches in our country, the World Council of Churches. It was amazing. We all agreed. The Council now speaks in my name. Listen!"

¤ WCC representatives continue: "In the name of the Protestants of the world, we, WCC, thank the president for his trust and our Roman Catholic brothers and sisters in the faith for their willingness to help. The Pope is ready to pay off the US government's debts and help everyone who owns dollars. There is only one demand. Anyone who would like to use his own money, must accept a payment card with the text 'Thanks and glory to the representative of the Roman Catholic Church and of the Son of God, Pope Francis'. We are supporting this. It's not difficult. There's no better solution. Otherwise, the world's dollars no longer will have any value."

Thus the beast, the Roman Catholic Church, and the mark of the beast, the Pope's payment card, are worshipped. And to the image of the beast, WCC, is given life by the president. Every US citizen is forced to believe in this false spiritual system, what is idolatry (4c§1317 and 6k§6(8)10, Rev. 13:14-15).

¤ Mixing politics and religion is against the US Constitution. The president shouldn't do something like that. And it is against God's law, what is unforgivable (Deu. 29:16-21).

At the same time, Satan enters into the president, whereby the USA becomes the seventh head of the beast. In this way, the president places himself in the WCC and pretends to be God {4b and 4c§1317, 2The. 2:(3b-)4, 7}.

The New Testament's Words Fury and Wrath

Shalom,
^ Almost as with the word hour, the words of God's fully-grown-wrath [orgé] and God's holy-fury [thumos] have been translated with many different words and confused (7e§67₁14, The Word Hour).
I would only use the words wrath and fury in the right places. For example, the meaning (and places) of the word wrath can be found with the link:
https://biblehub.com/greek/3709.htm
Prayer of them who look for God's Wisdom (cf. Eccl. 3:11), Bert

¤ Two thousand years ago, at the beginning of His ministry, Jesus Christ had announced the beginning of the Lord's acceptable era and had stopped where the prophet Isaiah had continued (cf. Lk. 4:19), Isa. 61:2a, <to proclaim (the year of the LORD's favor and) the day of our God's vengeance,>
The day of God's vengeance is the time of the Greater Tribulation, when the seventh trumpet has been blown and the Rapture has taken place (3e§12, Dan. 12:1-3; 5d§6(8)10, 1Cor. 15:51-52; 8a§89₁156, Rev. 11:15-19 and Mal. 4:1-6), Rev. 11:18, <".... The (Gentile) nations are in WRATH, and Your WRATH has come. The time has come to judge the dead and to reward Your servants the prophets, as well as the saints and those who fear Your name, both small and great—and to destroy those who destroy the earth.">
¤

¤ There are seven bowls of God's Fury. But in addition to the seventh bowl, He gives the system of Babylon the Great to drink the cup of His Wrath (Rev. 16:17-21), Rev. 16:19b, <And God remembered Babylon the great and gave her the cup of the wine of the fury of His WRATH.>
Wrath speaks of God's Final Judgment (Rev. 20:11-15), 1The. 1:10, <and to await His Son from heaven, whom He raised from the dead—Jesus our deliverer from the coming WRATH.>
¤ During his life, brother Branham had to warn about the mark of the beast (7d§67₁14, =), Rev. 14:9-13, < And a third messenger/angel followed them, calling out in a loud voice, "If anyone worships the beast and its image, and receives its mark on his forehead or on his hand, 10. he too will drink the wine of God's fury, poured undiluted into the cup of His WRATH. And he will be tormented in fire and sulfur in the presence of the holy angels and of the Lamb. 11. And the smoke of their torment rises forever and ever. Day and night there is no rest for those who worship the beast and its image, or for anyone who receives the mark of its name. ....">
At the end of the Greater tribulation time, the cup of God's Wrath is completely filled. It is a temporary Final Judgment. Partly happens what in the Final Judgment happens

when people's decisions have been made and it is no longer possible to change the course. Many get a taste of hell.

¤

¤ At the end of the church ages, there is the 'hour to harvest'. At the beginning of the hour is the Presence-Coming of our Lord Jesus, when He reaps His Harvest. And at the end of the harvest hour the era of the rulership of the Gentile nations ends {0c§Preface, 1The. 4:15-17; 6h§6(8)10, Mat. 24:3; 7e§67₁14, Rev. 14:15b (14-16)}, Mat. 13:37b-43, <"The One who sows the good seed is the Son of Man. 38. The field is the world, and the good seed represents the sons of the kingdom. The weeds are the sons of evil {/Evil}, 39. and the enemy who sows them is the devil. The harvest is the consummation of the age/era, and the harvesters are angels. 40. As the weeds are collected and burned in the fire, so will it be at the consummation of the age/era. 41. The Son of Man will send out His angels, and they will weed out of His kingdom every cause of sin and all who practice lawlessness. 42. And they will throw them into the fiery furnace, where there will be weeping and gnashing of teeth. 43. Then the righteous will shine like the sun in the kingdom of their Father. He who has ears, let him hear.">

The cup of the wine of the Fury of God's Wrath requires / is equal to blood, just as the red sameness of grapes and blood, and the wine-like preparation process can be found in the following text on the harvest of the earth. A huge number of people are going to die. The sea of blood of human beings can be found within a radius of about 184 miles (Rev. 14:17-20), Rev. 14:20, <And the winepress was trodden outside the city, and the blood that flowed from it rose as high as the bridles of the horses for a distance of 1,600 stadia.>

¤ The same Judgment is found of the end of the sixth seal, Rev. 6:15-17, <Then the kings of the earth, the nobles, the commanders, the rich, the mighty, and every slave and free man hid in the caves and among the rocks of the mountains. 16. And they said to the mountains and the rocks, "Fall on us and hide us from the face of the One seated on the throne, and from the WRATH of the Lamb. 17. For the great day of Their WRATH has come, and who is able to withstand it?">

And the same massacre is spoken of in the event when the Lord Jesus begins His Thousand Year Reign. The text in parentheses states that many bodies will be fed to the birds (Rev. 19:11-21), Rev. 19:15, <And from His mouth proceeds a sharp sword with which to strike down the nations, and He will rule them with an iron scepter. He treads the winepress of the fury of the WRATH of God the Almighty.>

¤ There is only one who saves us from the wrath to come, one Ark, one Body. The baptism of the Holy Ghost baptizes you/me into the Body of the Lord Jesus, Which will be raptured just before the Greater tribulation time (1Cor. 12:13).

God does not allow this Body to suffer a second time (cf. Heb. 6:6).

~ ~ ~

C9 (Revelation §8,9,11,15,16, Judgments Explained)

9f§89₁156

Ephesian/First Trumpet and Bowl (1s)

Shalom,
^ With trumpets and bowls is concentrated on the chapters 8, 9, 11, 15 and 16.
More of history and future is found with the prophecies of God's trumpets and bowls.
^ In this new series, I deal with the topics mainly from the point of view of local
churches and their believers. It differs from bBranham's line when in 1963 the Holy
Spirit led him to speak about seals from the perspective of Christendom as a whole.
Under the explanation of the fifth seal, I mentioned and discussed both approaches
(6h/6l§6(8)10).
Prayer of the servants who are preparing for the coming of their Lord (cf. Lk. 12:47),
Bert

1s: In the first church age, the believers' first love for God faded away.
It had been God's main rebuke to the believers of the Ephesian church age (Rev. 2:4).
¤ In his days, the apostle John had taught that our love for God is shown by how much
we love our brothers/sisters (1John 4:20-21).
There should be a readiness to die for each other as the Lord Jesus had been the
example for us. That is God's Love. On the other hand, among the believers, the main
problem had been the anti-Christian spirit in some of them according to the first seal,
what John had also spoken about (6l§6(8)10, 1John 2:18-19).
¤
1T1B: In 53 the revival of the church age of Ephesus had been born and in 170 the
Holy Spirit joined the next revival of the church age of Smyrna (6i§6(8)10, ChuRev).
In different churches, the revivals were dying out at different times. Sometime after
170, the last one went out. Then in Heaven the trumpet was blown (and the bowl was
poured out), and the lampstand of the Ephesian church was removed from its place
(1b§1-3/2b§45, Rev. 2:5).
1T: The symbol of the first heavenly angel's trumpet reads as follows, Rev. 8:7, <Then
the first {angel} sounded his trumpet, and hail and fire mixed with blood were hurled
down upon the earth. A third of the earth was burned up, along with a third of the trees
and all the green grass.>
The earth/land is once again the land of God's promise (cf. 3c§12, Rev. 12:15-16).
¤ It represented the churches of the Ephesian age. The trees and green grass
represented believers and their spiritual and physical children. Every believer would be
like a tree, Ps. 1:3, <He is like a tree planted by streams of water, yielding its fruit in
season, whose leaf does not wither, and who prospers in all he does.>

The judgment of the trumpet was directed at those believers who did not continue in the revival spirit, who did not continue hungry and thirsty for God's great works.

¤ Based on God's judgment, a third of the believers in the churches of the Ephesian age and all their children died spiritually. Without continuing the revival meetings no one came anymore to faith and God allowed a third of the believers to withdraw totally.

Blood represents both Salvation, and God's Judgment and death (Ex. 12:13).

¤ The believers in question had started to follow Jesus Christ and had potentially been spiritual people whose names had been in the Scroll of Life (Rev. 13:8b).

Having strayed from the hiking path of revival, a third part of them were erased from the Scroll of Life, (cf. Lk. 10:20), cf. Rev. 3:5, <"…. Like them, he who overcomes will be dressed in white. And I will never blot out his name from the Book of Life, but I will confess his name before My Father and His angels.">

¤

1B: On the same earth/land, that is, within the churches of the same died out revival, the fate of the name Christians was described. Together with the execution of the trumpet judgment, the first bowl was poured out (8c§89$_1$156, Rev. 8:5 and 15:7-8), Rev. 16:2, <So the first {angel} went and poured out his bowl on the earth, and loathsome, malignant sores broke out on those who had the mark of the beast and worshiped its image.>

Name Christians were not true believers at all. Their names had never been in the Book Scroll of Life. Outwardly they had been Christians. But inside they had not wanted to become spiritual Christians.

¤ By this bowl God opened the eyes of the surrounding people. Everywhere was noticed bad painful abscesses, unholy behavior of the Christians in question.

At that time, the beast was the state of the Roman emperors, and the image of the beast was the system of its idols. Not bowing to them would have meant big trouble. They had not been ready for that. They never had had such love that they had been ready to die for the Lord Jesus. It had been much easier to keep silent about Jesus and uncritically accept the 'culture' of that time. As a result, Satan had been able to mark with his mark those whose names from the beginning had not even been in the Scroll of Life. Their coming to faith was not ordained at all (3b§12, Acts 13:48).

Smyrnean/Second Trumpet and Bowl (2s)

Shalom,
^ Visiting the congregation and drinking the same Spirit of revival must have been an essential part of the lives of all believers throughout the ages of the churches. As we have been one body from the beginning (1Cor. 12:13).
And to the end (Heb. 10:25).
However, in the revival of the church age of Smyrna, it demanded everything.
Prayer of them who are looking for other believers, joint meetings and God's Revival until the end, Bert

1s: The first revival had had all the spiritual subtleties. As far as God was concerned, everything was perfect. But not on the side of believers. Their love had begun to fail.
According to the contents of the first seal, the main reasons for that would have been the anti-Christian spirit in some of the believers, as discussed last time (9f§89₁156, 1John 2:18-19).
¤ This information would have helped the true believers to continue and be able to hold revival meetings and love each other. According to the apostle John, at some point those antichrist believers would have left.
On the other hand, one revival has never been self-evident. In churches, new generations are born and the former ones die away. Of the children of the new generations, each must separately seek God and convert and be baptized in water and seek the baptism of the spirit (Acts 2:38-40).
¤
2s: When Love for other believers and for God had faded, God chose a more imperfect revival. But the revival where His Love was again.
The Smyrnean church age revival lasted from 170 to ~312 (6i§6(8)10, ChuRev).
¤ When you read the message of Jesus Christ to the messenger of the church in Smyrna, you will not find anything negative to say. But the challenges had been hard (Rev. 2:9-11), Rev. 2:9-10, <I know your affliction and your poverty—though you are rich! And I am aware of the slander of those who falsely claim to be Jews, but {are} in fact a synagogue of Satan. 10. Do not fear what you are about to suffer. Look, the devil is about to throw some of you into prison to test you, and you will suffer tribulation for ten days. Be faithful even unto death, and I will give you the crown of life.>
Very harsh conditions lasted until the start of the Pergamon revival in 312 AD. Then times in the Roman Empire became easier (6i§6(8)10, Emperor Constantine).
¤ Previously, the anti-Christian spirit in some believers had been a problem. The contents of the second seal revealed an anti-Christian spirit in some of the church

leaders, who got along better with the local political leaders than with the revival believers (6l§6(8)10, 2s).

Holding regular revival meetings had been a challenge for the believers. Especially for the leaders who were usually the first to be punished.

¤

2T: After the revival of the Smyrnean church had died out, the judgment of the trumpet sounded like this, Rev. 8:8-9, <Then the second angel sounded his trumpet, and something like a great mountain burning with fire was thrown into the sea. A third of the sea turned to blood, 9. a third of the living creatures in the sea died, and a third of the ships were destroyed.>

The symbol of the trumpet speaks of spiritual believers who did not participate in organizing the revival meetings of their own church. That is why they had lived as if in the sea, among worldly people (cf. Rev. 17:15).

¤ A third of the believers in question had to die spiritually according to the judgment of the trumpet. For example, like Judas Iscariot, the betrayer of our Lord (Ps. 69:25), Acts 1:20a, <"For it is written in the book of Psalms: 'May his place be deserted; let there be no one to dwell in it,' ....">

In the same context it is said (Ps. 69:22-28), Ps. 69:28, <May they be blotted out of the Book of Life and not listed with the righteous.>

¤ And the same fate befell a third of them, who had lived as if on a ship.

They had attended the revivals in different groups, but were not committed to one group. That was not acceptable to God either.

¤

2B: Together with the trumpet the plague of the second bowl was poured out, Rev. 16:3, <And the second {angel} poured out his bowl into the sea, and it turned to blood like that of one dead, and every living soul in the sea died.>

The bowl speaks of a plague for the name Christians who had not been spiritual believers at all. Not one of them had constructively participated in the revival of their own congregation. Each of them had lived as in the sea, in the world (cf. Rev. 17:15).

¤ Each of them was a human being. That's why is talked about living souls.

Those who were outside the revival were already dead in God's eyes while living (cf. 1Tim. 5:6).

Pergamean/Third Trumpet and Bowl (3s)

Shalom,
3s: The revival of the church of Pergamos began in 312/313 AD. with the Edict of Nantes/Milan, when the emperor of the Western and Eastern Roman Empire Constantine (emperor 306–337) proclaimed freedom of religion. Suddenly there was more freedom. That is how the type of the revival of the church of Smyrna changed (6l§6(8)10, 3s).
No longer there was an immediate death threat. Although other challenges appeared. According to the message of the black horse symbol of the third seal, the main problem from then on was that at the local level anti-Christian political leaders began to manipulate the believers (6l§6(8)10, 3s).
2S: From 312 to 1520 from the point of view of the entire Christian society, the anti-Christian spirit was embodied in the leading Roman Catholic chief bishops and popes, with whom the kings of the earth committed fornication. It was the large-scale explanation of the secret of the second seal in the church ages of Pergamos and Thyatira (6i§6(8)10, ChuRev).
1S: Already in the beginning of the church in Rome, it had departed from the truth and adopted all sorts of pagan customs, when in 41 AD. the emperor Claudius had expelled e.g. the Jewish believers from this city.
Prayer of them who believe they are living in the last moments of the churches (Dan. 12:4), Bert

3T: The fourth revival (of Thyatira) began in 606 and shortly thereafter the last Pergamos' revivals died out. Then the third trumpet was blown (6i§6(8)10, ChuRev), Rev. 8:10-11, <Then the third angel sounded his trumpet, and a great star burning like a torch fell from heaven and landed on a third of the rivers and on the springs of water. 11. The name of the star is Wormwood. A third of the waters turned bitter like wormwood oil, and many people died from the bitter waters.>
Here we are talking about streams and their sources, that is fresh water. Fresh streams of water in the New Testament speak of God's Word. Jesus Christ had told the Samaritan woman that He could give her living water (John 4:10).
¤ It is living water that becomes a well of water in a person and springs up to eternal life (John 4:14; Rev. 22:17).
This water cleansed this sinful woman and turned into living water in her. But it was not yet a complete conversion. The baptism of the Holy Spirit had not yet been. The Holy Ghost had not yet come.
¤ In the Pergamos' revival similar believers were spiritual potential believers whose names had been in the Lamb's Book of Life. God's Word had cleansed them. But many

did not fully accept God's Word. Streams and water sources had been part of God's land, part of the foundation of the Word and Its Promises, in this case the churches of the revival (cf. 3c§12, Rev. 12:15-16).

Likewise, many priests had spoken in manners approved by the state. It had been an incomplete gospel. Therefore the Lord Jesus had spoken to the messenger of Pergamos as the two-edged sharp Word of God (Heb. 4:12 and Rev. 2:12).

¤ The star messenger of the Pergamean church age, Martin, had been a soldier who, after his conversion, had become the bishop of Tours (6i§6(8)10, ChuRev).

Seen from the outside, the progress in this church age had been astonishing. With the sympathy of the emperor and the state, many and large groups gathered. But God knows who among them had been fully surrendered and ready to receive the final Seal of the Holy Spirit, and who was not (Eph. 4:30).

¤ In the end, those waters ended in the sea, what is masses of worldly human beings, without being born from above (cf. Rev. 17:15).

God condemned these kinds of believers in letting the streams and springs of God's Word become bitter and salty, like the sea. By bitterness and other pressures many believers fell away and died spiritually, Heb. 12:15, <See to it that no one falls short of the grace of God, and that no root of bitterness springs up to cause trouble and defile many.>

¤

3B: The third bowl tells about name Christians in the streams and springs of the Pergamean church age, Rev. 16:4-7, <And the third {angel/messenger} poured out his bowl into the rivers and springs of water, and they turned to blood. 5. And I heard the angel/messenger of the waters say: "Righteous are You, O Holy One, who is and was, because You have brought these judgments. 6. For they have spilled the blood of saints and prophets, and You have given them blood to drink, as they deserve." 7. And I heard the altar reply: "Yes, Lord God Almighty, true and just {are} Your judgments.">

To these name Christians the streams and water sources became completely poisonous. They had not supported the revivals at all. Instead, they had participated in killing saints and prophets of the revival. For this God informed us that it will never be forgiven. Their future place is the lake of fire (Rev. 20:15).

¤ Outside of the revival had been Satan's throne (Revelation 2:13a).

Saints and prophets had had to fight amid the leaders of darkness. But in the name and faith of Jesus they had overcome (Rev. 2:13).

Thyatirean/Fourth Trumpet and Bowl (4s)

Shalom,
Prayer of them who know that by fearing God we receive extraordinary grace (Ps. 103:11), Bert

4s: The revival of the fourth church, the Thyatirean revival, began in 606 (6i§6(8)10, ChuRev).
The spiritual background of the fourth seal taught the believers of the local churches the brutality of life. Europe was living in dark ages. Only the religion led by the popes was allowed and any other way of believing was forbidden. Around the believers was but death. All kinds of persecutions were everywhere (6l§6(8)10, 4s).
¤ Each believer stood spiritually completely alone and depended on God from beginning to end.
There were no other options. Someone was a believer and lived to the fullest, or he was not a believer. Every now and then someone had to confess to being a black sheep and be prepared to suffer the consequences.
4T: After a very long time and after entire nations had become ripe for it, the revival of the fifth church age, the Reformation revival, was born in 1520 (6i§6(8)10, ChuRev).
Almost at the same time, the trumpet of the fourth age sounded in Heaven. The judgments of the earlier trumpets had targeted lazy (Jewish and Gentile) believers. But outside of personal revivals, there had not been anymore other church directions. That is one of the reasons why the spiritual war of the next trumpet (and the spiritual wars of the following trumpets) now only targeted the Jews, Rev. 8:12, <Then the fourth angel sounded his trumpet, and a third of the sun and moon and stars were struck. A third of the stars were darkened, a third of the day was without light, and a third of the night as well.>
¤ Previously I had discussed that by means of the sun and the moon and the twelve stars God had spoken of His original chosen people. However, now is talked about many stars in addition to the sun and the moon (cf. 3a§12, Gen. 37:9-10).
Yet is talked about the same people. It can be understood in the following way:
¤
= "In the times of Abraham, Isaac and Jacob, their descendants were seen as a nation of twelve tribes/stars. But believers are also called stars in the Bible. Thus, when Jesus Christ was crucified, there were already many more believers of the Jewish people (e.g. Gen. 15:5 and Dan. 12:3b).
¤ Since the birth of Jesus, the dragon / old serpent / Devil / Satan was focused on destroying Him (Rev. 12:9a), Rev. 12:4b, <And the dragon stood before the woman who was about to give birth, ready to devour her child as soon as she gave birth.>
First, it had sought to kill Him through King Herod (Mat. 2:13-23).

¤ Then it had personally tried to get hold of Him when Jesus began his ministry (Lk. 4:1-13).

Then, before the crucifixion, it had found Jesus' disciple Judas, into whom it had entered (3c§12, John 13:27a).

¤ Next, it had found the spiritual leaders of the Jewish people, under whose leadership the Jewish people had cried out (Mat. 27:15-26), Mat. 27:25, <"His blood be on us and on our children!">

The people made a huge mistake, by which the dragon caught many in his hands. Then a third of the possible believers of that time, the stars of heaven, died in their sins (cf. John 8:24), Rev. 12:4a, <His [dragon's] tail swept a third of the stars from the sky, tossing them to the earth.>" =

¤

4T: In this way, it can be believed that the judgment of the fourth trumpet speaks of the same entire Jewish people who lived in exile at that time. God permitted that everywhere the pressures and the temptations increased, so that in that time period a third of the Jewish people, a third of the sun, and a third of the moon, and a third of the stars, forsook its roots. This part left the Jewish way of life, leaving their other relatives alone and under greater assimilation pressures. It was part of the sanctification process of the remaining Jews (e.g. 7d§67$_1$14, Zec. 13:9a).

Of course, the small part of them who received Jesus Christ as their personal Saviour did not leave its roots at all.

¤

4B: Together with the judgment of the fourth trumpet, the plague of the fourth bowl began, Rev. 16:8-9, <Then the fourth {angel} poured out his bowl on the sun, and it was given power to scorch the people with fire. 9. And the people were scorched by intense heat, and they cursed the name of God, who had authority over these plagues; yet they did not repent and give Him glory.>

With the Reformation, God let His living Word become very bright, what scorched all name Christians outside of the Sardisean church revival. They had no chance to defend themselves against the new teaching of the Reformation. Just as God and His Word can be compared to the sun, while the stars/believers reflect the light of the sun (also Rev. 1:20).

Sardisean/Fifth Trumpet and Bowl (5s)

Shalom,
^ With the history of humanity and especially of us believers the Book Revelation deals. The same all the believers together would be barely able to write in retrospect. But imagine. God wrote this history in advance, before the foundation of the world, so that He would be feared (cf. Rev. 13:8b / Eccl. 3:14-15).
Prayer of them who obey the gospel (1Pet. 4:17), Bert

5s5T: The fifth Sardisean church age, the Reformation revival, began in 1520 and ended somewhere after 1750 (6i§6(8)10, ChuRev).
When all the revivals of the Reformation had ended, the fifth trumpet was blown.
567T123W: Then, in addition to the trumpets, the fifth seal speaks solely of the Jewish people. The content of the secret of this seal began to become clear to the Jews who had come to faith (6l§6(8)10, 5sS; and 7a§67₁14, 5sS).
Both the last three trumpets and the three woe-cries / world wars belong together (and literally drive the right Israelites back to God and to the land of Israel) (7c and 7d§67₁14).
¤
5T: The trumpet's symbol said, Rev. 9:1-6, <Then the fifth angel sounded his trumpet, and I saw a star that had fallen from heaven to earth, and it was given the key to the pit of the Abyss. 2. The star opened the pit of the Abyss, and smoke rose out of it like the smoke of a great furnace, and the sun and the air were darkened by the smoke from the pit. 3. And out of the smoke, locusts descended on the earth, and they were given power like that of the scorpions of the earth. 4. They were told not to harm the grass of the earth or any plant or tree, but only those who did not have the seal of God on their foreheads. 5. They [locusts] were not given power to kill them, but only to torment them for five months, and their torment was like the stinging of a scorpion. 6. In those days men will seek death and will not find it; they will long to die, but death will escape them.>
In the Book Revelation, a star represents a believer in whom the Holy Spirit lives or a person who is on his way to be born from above. And a fallen star represents a believer who has spiritually died (cf. 9i§89₁156, Gen. 37:9-10).
¤ From this time on, in different parts of the world, one or a few spiritually dead believers received an innumerable amount of demons at their disposal. That's how God simply allowed it.
Usually grasshoppers eat grass and plants and trees, but it was forbidden. Instead, they were supposed to harm people without killing them. People who did not have the Seal of God on their foreheads. That is, every person who was not (yet) born a child of God by breathing the Holy Spirit (cf. Eph. 1:13-14).

¤ A scorpion's lifespan is five months, so these scorpions are dangerous from beginning to end. The followers of the founders of such a false gospel learned from the beginning to spread the same heresies in the streets and everywhere. Likewise, each of their disciples learned from the beginning to approach other people. It has affected societies in such a way that the meaning of life has been increasingly lost. The Content and Hope of God's Word have been darkening and disappearing. People long for death, yet 'death will escape them'.

Examples of believers and their organizations that arose at that time and have continued to act fearlessly to this day include: Ellen G. White (1827-1915) and the Seventh-day Adventist Church, Joseph Smith Jr. (1805-1844) and his Mormon organization, Charles Taze Russell (1852-1916) and Jehovah's Witnesses.

¤ They predicted things for which there is no biblical ground, but for which apparent explanations have been found.

In the same period Charles R. Darwin (1809-1882) had grown up, who developed his evolution theory. It has become a belief of scientists (and all), who do not want to believe in God. Any colleague or science publisher who writes something against it, is threatened with excommunication, exclusion of research work, or being boycotted.

¤

1W: God used those 'believers' possessed by locust demons to challenge unprepared Jewish (and Christian) believers. But when the First World War ended at God's 11th hour, at 11 a.m. on 11/11/1918, all the living and future 144,000 Israelites were sealed (cf. 7c§67$_1$14, Rev. 7:1-3 and 4-8).

The plague of the fifth trumpet judgment can still be noted in the world, but because the sealing neutralized its direct influence on the Israelites, it was said, Rev. 9:12a, <.... The first woe has passed. ....>

¤

5B: When the fifth trumpet was blown, the fifth bowl was simultaneously poured out, Rev. 16:10-11, <And the fifth {angel} poured out his bowl on the throne of the beast, and its kingdom was plunged into darkness, and men began to gnaw their tongues in anguish 11. and curse the God of heaven for their pains and sores; yet they did not repent of their deeds.>

After the Reformation, the kingdom of the beast continued to operate through the Roman Catholic Church. But then its members were shocked. God allowed tremendous criticism to rise up against them. It was generally observed that the leaders of that church and its members were not living as holy a life as it should have been. All kinds of spiritual abscesses, all kinds of unholy behavior, were noticed. It caused a lot of pain. However, there was no readiness within the Roman Catholic Church to change its ways.

Philadelphian/Sixth Trumpet and Bowl (6s)

Shalom,
6s: During the Philadelphian church age, the secrets of the sixth seal began to unveil (7a§67₁14, 6sS).
Prayer of them who know that all kingdoms and times are in God's Hands (Acts 1:6-7), Bert

56T1W: Last time I dealt among others with the first Woe, the First World War. It was reported to be part of the fifth trumpet period. However, the nature of the judgment of this trumpet was a mere spiritual plague. Therefore, it should be understood that the woe of the fifth trumpet was also part of the sixth trumpet.

The sixth trumpet can be called the killing plague of the Jewish people. The judgment of this trumpet was carried out after the last revivals of the Philadelphian church age died out, sometime after 1906 (6i§6(8)10, ChuRev).

6T: In 1914 it was implemented. From the Euphrates river are found four killing angels, which let the First World War start, and of which was spoken in the seventh chapter (7c§67₁14, Rev. 7:1-3), Rev. 9:13-15, < And the sixth angel sounded {his} trumpet: and I heard a voice from the four horns of the golden altar which {is} before God, 14. saying to the sixth angel that had the trumpet, Loose the four angels which are bound at the great river Euphrates. 15. And the four angels were loosed, who are prepared for the hour and day and month and year, that they might slay the third part of men;>

The holiness revival of Philadelphia had been enormous and mighty. Therefore, it took its own time before this revival of brotherly love died out everywhere. But it went out because the gifts of the Holy Spirit were rejected. As the Lord Jesus had announced: power was little (1b§1-3, Rev. 3:7-13, and especially verse 8).

6B: The plague of the sixth bowl was poured out at the same time, at the beginning of the First World War, Revelation 16:12, <And the sixth poured out his bowl on the great river Euphrates; and its water was dried up, that the way of the kings from the rising of the sun might be prepared.>

It is the same spiritual Euphrates. At one time God had promised the Israelites up to the Euphrates as their territory (cf. Joshua 1:4).

4S6B: As this stream dries up, nothing prevents the Jewish people in Israel and the land of Israel from being harassed by political powers from the direction of the sunrise, from the north and the east, as it has been seen many times since 1914 until this day. In addition to that, under the plague of the sixth bowl three unclean frog spirits appear, which I dealt with under the fourth seal. These will mislead and gather the rulers of the world into the final war of Armageddon (6k§6(8)10, Rev. 16:13-16).

The bowls are the plagues that God intended for the name Christians. That is how the next prophecy of the prophet Zechariah is meaningful. At the end of the time of the greater tribulation, all the nations of the world together, including the United States, will attack Jerusalem and Israel (7d§67₁14, Zec. 12:1-3).

¤ In addition, they will kill the two witnesses of God on the streets of Jerusalem (7b§67₁14, Rev. 11:1---7).

For states with a Christian history, this attack is a fatal mistake. Just as God once held the Jewish people responsible for rejecting Jesus Christ. The (former) Christian states should have understood that the central role of the Gentiles in God's plan of salvation has been temporary. After that, it is again the turn of the people of Israel to proclaim the gospel with power (3b§12, Rm. 11:25b-27).

¤ The text of the letter to the Romans says that at some point the believers of the Gentile church ages are taken to Heaven and after that all Israel will be saved. Of the city of Jerusalem Jesus Christ had given a similar prophecy, Lk. 21:24b, <"…. and Jerusalem shall be trodden down of {the} nations until {the} times of {the} nations be fulfilled.">

Unfortunately, when Israel took over East Jerusalem, and the Judea and Samaria area's in the Six Day War of 1967, all the nations of the world, including the United States, dictated that Israel was its occupier.

¤

¤ Communism is God's tool in this end time. God will use Russia, China and eight other dictator nations coming from the sunrise, the horns of the beast, to destroy Babylon the Great in one hour (7e§67₁14, Rev. 17:12).

The harlot Great Babylon represents in the first place the Roman Catholic Church, followed by the churches of the Reformation, as well as at the end by the other Protestants {4abc§1317, Rev. 17:5 / 17:(1-)7)}.

¤ These dictatorships will be at the end of the Greater tribulation period the only remaining world powers, which will then be disciplined {ten horns, ten toes, Dan. 2:(19-)42(-45), (4a§1317)}, Rev. 17:13-14, <These have one mind, and give their power and authority to the beast. 14. These shall make war with the Lamb, and the Lamb shall overcome them; for he is Lord of lords and King of kings: and they {that are} with him called, and chosen, and faithful.>

The First World War was needed to transform Russia into a communist state. The war against Germany caused great military losses and as a result the army had begun to revolt. After that, the Bolsheviks and other socialist groups carried out the 1917-revolution. Then the hour-long political period/reign of the ten dictators began, whose king of the north is Russia (Dan. 11:40).

Laodicean/Seventh Trumpet and Bowl (7s)

Shalom,

6T: I continue with the sixth trumpet (and bowl). This period began in 1914 (9k§89₁156).

During that time, a third of the Jewish people will be killed. However, only God knows the real totals of the Jewish people and when that prophesy will be fulfilled (Rev. 9:18; 9i§89₁156, Rev. 8:12).

^ During the Second World War, e.g. because of the persecutions of Hitler and Stalin some 6 million of the 18 million were killed. In that way God gave the Jews throughout the world the longing to return to and establish their own land, by which they would get the possibility to defend themselves (cf. 8b§89₁156, Jer. 16:14-16).

Yet, the purpose of the sixth trumpet, the honoring of God, had not yet been accomplished (Rev. 9:20-21).

Only after the earthquake and seven thousand more victims it will be fulfilled (7b§67₁14, Rev. 11:11-14).

7T: Next awaits the purpose of the seventh trumpet, the coming to faith of all Israel.

Prayer of them who want to see the signs of our time (cf. Mat. 16:2-4), Bert

7s7T: At the end of the Laodicean church age, the seventh trumpet will be blown, what ends the Silence of the Seventh Seal and initiates the Rapture {4a§1317, 1The. 4:15; 5d and 6m§6(8)10, 7s, Rev. (7:9-)8:1}.

It is the beginning of the most important event of the end-time (Rev. 11:15-19), Rev. 11:15b, <"The kingdom of the world of our Lord and of his Christ is come, and he shall reign to the ages of ages.">

67B: At the same time the last bowl shall be poured out (Rev. 16:17-21), Rev. 16:17, <And the seventh {angel} poured out his bowl on the air; and there came out a great voice from the temple of the heaven, from the throne, saying, It is done.>

'It is done' confirms this major end-time event, as also mentioned under the symbol of the sixth bowl (Rev. 16:12-16), Rev. 16:15, <"Behold, I am coming like a thief. Blessed is the one who remains awake and clothed, so that he will not go naked and let his shame be exposed.">

7T6B: On the opposite, on earth begins the day of God's vengeance, the time of the Greater tribulation. The wrath of the nations is seen first (also 6Bowl) and then the Wrath of God (8e§89₁156, Rev. 11:18).

After 1260 days, many nations will jointly attack Jerusalem, Israel, and God's plan. It is the war of Armageddon (7d§67₁14, Sak. 14:1-2a; 9k§89₁156, Rev. 16:(13-)16).

6T7B: Then strikes the earthquake of the sixth trumpet in Jerusalem, which is also mentioned in the symbol of the seventh bowl (cf. 7e§67₁14; Rev. 11:11---14), Rev.

16:18-19, <And there were lightnings, and voices, and thunders; and there was a great earthquake, such as was not since men were upon the earth, such an earthquake, so great. 19. And the great city was {divided} into three parts; and the cities of the nations fell: and great Babylon was remembered before God to give her the cup of the wine of the fury of his wrath.>

Not only will Jerusalem go into three parts, throughout the world the cities will fell.

7T3W: Every country is in a terrible chaos. But the West probably the most of all. Then the ten dictatorial states will suddenly see a good opportunity to attack and burn the system of the harlot Great Babylon (9k§89$_1$156, communism), Rev. 17:16, <And the ten horns that you saw, and the beast, these will hate the harlot, and will make her desolate and naked, and will eat her flesh, and burn her with fire;>

Communism has been God's weapon. Since 1917 it was used to impoverish the West. Gradually our factories, money, planning, influence, etc. have been relocated to the lands of communism and its sphere of influence. At the end is the final stage, the third Woe / World War, the execution of the judgment of the seventh trumpet. It is the fire baptism of the earth (2Pet. 3:7).

¤ Next, the Jewish people will notice that their nearby support states have been destroyed. Now it's totally left alone. With only one chance of escape left. Suddenly it is ready to cry with one mouth for the help of the Lord of the Mount of Olives, Jesus Christ (7d§67$_1$14, Zec. 13:8---14:4a).

Then everyone whose name is in God's book, will be ready to accept the Lord Jesus as Saviour and Leader. In one day a nation is born from above (Dan. 12:1 and John 3:3).

¤ At the end of 45 days, in great Light and Power, Jesus will appear (7e§67$_1$14, Dan. 12:11-12/13).

The purpose of the seventh trumpet will be accomplished, and the Ark of God's Covenant will become visible for all the people of Israel (Rev. 11:19).

¤ At the beginning of the Greater tribulation time for a big part of the people of Israel It was still covered (Rev. 11:2).

Now God's way into the Holy Places has been opened to them (7a§67$_1$14, Heb. 9:8).

¤

7B: The execution of the last bowl is a plague for all nations, what starts with the Third World War (Rev. 16:19b).

At the same time it will be seen that God has begun to protect the citizens of the land of Israel. Blindness, rotting of the flesh, chaos, etc., affect other nations but not the people of Israel (Zec. 12:4 and 14:12-15).

¤ The seas, rivers, islands and mountains will explode by atomic and hydrogen bombs and disappear, and earth's surfaces and atmospheres will be changed completely (Sak. 14:18; Rev. 16:20 and cf. Rev. 21:1b).

The ensuing blanket of steam and smoke will block the sun's light and heat, and a new ice age will start (after the ice ages of the Noachian flood). Then hailstones weighing about 114 pounds (= a talent) will begin to rain (Rev. 16:21).

~ ~ ~

"WHY, HOW AND WHO?"

Shalom,
^ At the end, every nation that has attacked Jerusalem and Israel and opposed His Plan, God will stone. It is the last Bowl Plague (9l§89₁156, 7K, Revelation 16:20 and 16:21).
As under the Old Testament adulterers should be stoned (Deu. 22:20-24; John 8:3-11).
^ After that, in the last thousand years of the earth God will use water to discipline all the gentile nations. If one people does not honor the LORD of hosts, it will not rain there. Even the people of Egypt, who receive a big part of their water from the Nile, will not receive water {Zec. 14:(16-)18(-19) (7d§67₁14; 9l§89₁156)}.
At the same time not a single unholy thing or person is allowed to be in God's Temple (Zec. 14:20-21).
Prayer of them who know that man proposes, but God disposes (cf. Prov. 16:9), Bert

¤ In the book Revelation every believer is in a mighty voice warned about a system, that in the time of the church ages would be very beautiful on the outside but very polluted on the inside (Rev. 18).
Throughout the years but especially for our end-time God has warned, Rev. 18:4-5, <"Come out of her, My people, so that you will not share in her sins or contract any of her plagues. 5. For her sins are piled up to heaven, and God has remembered her iniquities. ….">
¤ The last verse of chapter 17 reveals that Rome, the state of the popes, is the great city whose spiritual name is Babylon the Great (4a§1317; Rev. 13:3a and 17:7, 9, 18). Once upon a time the city of Rome, the Roman Empire, had turned into the Rome of the popes. The strongest empire ever known was finally wounded to death. But under the reign of emperor Constantine it came back to life. And from about the year 1500 in colonialism, it has penetrated the whole world, adapting to all sorts of forms of local idolatry (8d§89₁156, Rev. 13:3a).
¤ This is how in its deadly religious and commercial power, it has ruled as a goddess and used kings and merchants until the present time. It had been the original church of Rome, which had been badly lost from the beginning (9h§89₁156, 2S and 1S).
The first bishops considered themselves more important than the Word. They told people that they could forgive their sins. This was never true. Man's sins are not forgiven through men, but by water baptism in the name of Jesus Christ (cf. Acts 2:38).

¤ These false apostles and superior spiritual leaders (Nicolaitans) were still opposed in the first revival of the church age of Ephesus, but less and less after that (Rev. 2:2, 6). Significantly Babylon the Great has been called the mother of the prostitutes and of the abominations of the earth. She is a woman who has broken her marriage vow to God in infidelity. She left, committing adultery with kings and at the end with the devil. The daughters, born from them, are like her (4b ja 4c§1317, Rev. 17:5).

¤ These, the Protestants, quickly organized themselves in the same lifeless manner as the church from which they had left. Belonging to the same spiritual society would be the most important deed. And they soon will decide that literally connecting with the pope and his church and his sign will be ok (6k§6(8)10/8d§89₁156, Rev. 12:13).

In the end-time of our churches, every believer must leave the wrongly organized churches and congregations. This has been preached by brother Branham until boredom (cf. 7d§67₁14, Rev. 14:9-13).

¤

¤ Once upon a time God had given the cities and regions of Sodom and Gomorrah as warning examples, Judas 7, <In like manner, Sodom and Gomorrah and the cities around them, who indulged in sexual immorality and pursued strange flesh, are on display as an example of those who sustain the punishment of eternal fire.>

From a global perspective, especially in our Christian Western countries, men and women are changing their gender roles, and sexuality has become an object of worship. Sodomic laws have been pushed through. Therefore, God's fire and wrath awaits especially them when the true believers have been taken to heaven (1Pet. 4:17).

¤ At the time of Sodom and Gomorrah mankind had not yet figured out how to burn up cities and countries. Thus God destroyed them independently, Gen. 19:24, <Then the LORD rained down sulfur and fire on Sodom and Gomorrah—from the LORD out of the heavens.>

But at the end of our church ages atomic and hydrogen bombs etc. have been invented. God's Greatness is seen in the fact that already two thousand years ago He announced why and how and through whom He allows those burning destruction weapons to be used.

¤ First, (former) Christian states along with other states in the world are attacking Israel and Jerusalem. Eitherway, every Christian should have known, that it is against God's Plan. That land and capital God promised to the descendants of Abraham and David (Gen. 15:18-21 and Mat. 5:35).

Therefore, the ten dictator states of communism will then be allowed to burn them (9k and 9l§89₁156, Rev. 17:16).

¤ In this way the 'destroyer' who two thousand years ago strengthened a 'covenant' with many against Jesus Christ and His followers, is destroyed (3d§12, Dan. 9:26-27 and Mat. 27:22).

And after 'the consumption and what is determined, is poured on the destroyer' the whole people of Israel will come to faith {9l§89₁156, Zec. 13:8---14:4a}.

~ ~ ~

C11 (Revelation §19,20,21,22, Kingdom of God)

11a§19-22

Millennial Sabbath Kingdom of Christ

Shalom,
^ What is God's coming solution to the climate problem? Why does He allow Russian cruelty?
God works explicitly according to His Own Word. He is not affected by it, that almost every person or believer on earth today disagrees with Him. His Plans and Answers can be found in the Bible.
But in what do we believe more? In our feelings or in what God has foretold?
^ Physical wars, famines, earthquakes, all must have happened (cf. Mat. 24:6-7).
Because wars are, at their deepest, spiritual wars (Eph. 6:12).
Prayer of them, who are clothed with all the armor of God (Eph. 6:11), Bert

¤ During the Greater Tribulation the beast with the seven heads speaks great words and blasphemies against God {4a§1317 and 7a and 7b§67₁14, Revelation 13:5(-6)}.
At the beginning of these 42 months the United States becomes its seventh head (cf. 7b§67₁14, Rev. 12:13).
¤ At the same time the United States gets involved in persecuting believers. These are specifically the Messianic believers who keep the commandments of God and have the testimony of Jesus {7d§67₁14, Rev. 12:17 (12b---17); 14:12 (9-13)}.
Two of them are the witnesses who preach and prophesy in Jerusalem. The other ones are the 144,000 Israelites, who meet them and come with their help to faith in the Lord Jesus (7b§67₁14, Rev. 11:1-6).
¤ Two witnesses preach e.g. against the mark of the beast, which is the papal payment card, and which will be introduced under the auspices of the United States throughout the world (8d§89₁156, mark of the beast).
E.g. therefore the president of the United States does not like them. However, the witnesses strike with plagues at anyone who tries to stop them. It makes all nations increasingly angry (Rev. 11:5-6).
¤ After coming to faith 144,000 will travel all over the world to evangelize and warn of the mark of the beast. The mark of the beast means eternal death for everyone who takes it (!) (Rev. 14:9-13), Rev. 14:11, <".... And the smoke of their torment rises forever and ever. Day and night there is no rest for those who worship the beast and its image, or for anyone who receives the mark of its name. ....">
The 144,000 are easy targets for Satan and his powers. But it doesn't bother them (Rev. 14:13).
¤

¤ At His first Coming, Jesus Christ paid the ransom of mankind (1Tim. 2:6).

The second time He will fetch His Bride's Church in the cloudy upper air (1The. 4:13-17).

¤ The third time He will rule the world in the last/seventh thousand (sabbath) years together with His Bride (Rev. 20:1-6).

Before His last Coming both the land of Israel and the whole earth will tremble. Simultaneously Jerusalem falls into three parts and its terrain changes greatly (9l§89₁156, Rev. 16:18-19).

¤ The temple mountain in Jerusalem, where the two Islamic mosques stood, becomes a great valley (7b§67₁14; Zec. 14:3-5 and 10-11).

Next the third world war will be started with among others atomic bombs. It suddenly changes the attitude of the people of Israel. Thus, as a whole nation, it cries out to the Lord Jesus for help (9l§89₁156, Zec. 13:8---14:4).

¤ Only Russia, as well as the other nine dictators, have the cruelty to start using weapons, that could potentially destroy the entire earth. However, the destruction is the result of the spiritual decline of the West (10a§18, Jude 7).

Ten dictators carry out God's judgment on the states represented by the whore Babylon the Great, where a democratic form of government has replaced Christianity.

¤ At the same time the fire baptism of the earth will resolve the climate crisis.

Under the shadow of smoke and steam anew ice age begins. Hailstones bomb most of the human inventions into pieces. The temperature of the earth's surface is dropping permanently many degrees (9l§89₁156, Rev. 16:21).

¤ Not only the Temple Mount has disappeared. A new much higher mountain has risen up, from where on its slope Jerusalem is visible at a distance of almost 20 kilometers (Ezek. 40:2, 43:1-12, and 45:1-8).

The mountain and the city area and the terrain have just become suitable for the instructions how to build the temple and the city and the landscape as described by the prophet Ezekiel in his time (Ezek. 40-48).

¤ When the western states have been burned to the ground, only the eastern states are somehow still existing (9l§89₁156, Rev. 17:16).

About them the Bible talks with e.g. the names of Gog and Magog in the prophecies of Ezekiel (Ezek. 38 and 39).

¤ Due to the pollution by the atomic bombs and after the bombing with the ice balls, Ezekiel also gave an accurate picture of the losses of those states (Ezek. 38:1-7 and §39).

Everything would have been a big warning. But at the end of the millennial sabbath kingdom a large portion of the same crowd will again attack Israel and Jerusalem. Then the other prophecies of Ezekiel for Gog and Magog will be fulfilled. Then God Himself completely destroys the invaders. Nothing is left behind (Rev. 20:7-9).

New Heaven and New Earth

Shalom,
^ Every Christian should pray for the Jews and Israel. It is according to God's plan (Rm. 11:11-12).
In that way, both they and we are blessed with the blessing of father Abraham (Gen. 12:3 and Acts 3:25).
Prayer for the Jewish people and the land of Israel, Bert

¤ A great plan had been prepared for the people of the twelve tribes. It gave already birth to the Saviour of mankind, what has been a great sign for the whole world (3a§12, Rev. 12:1, 2 and 5).
But, God's second goal, the becoming of His personal Bride, did not (yet) succeed. God even separated from His people and has sought a New Bride throughout the world (3b§12, Mat. 22:1-14).
¤ When the people of Israel had become a nation and had left the land of Egypt, God had given the tribe of Levi the task of taking care of the Tabernacle and all its affairs (Numb. 1).
At the same time, God had divided the tribes into five parts. In the center the tribe of Levi. On the east side the front tribes of Judah, Issachar and Zebulon. On the south side, the tribes of Reuben, Simeon and Gad. On the west side, the tribes of Ephraim, Manasseh, and Benjamin. And on the north side the tribes of Dan, Asser, and Naphtali (Numb. 2).
¤ The number of each tribe had to be counted, but not of the tribe of Levi. To the others were given parts of the land, but the inheritance of the tribe of Levi was the Lord, the God of Israel {Jos. 13:(1-)33}.
Therefore, a thirteenth tribe had been needed, obtained through the sons of Joseph, Ephraim and Manasseh (Gen. 48).
¤
¤ When God speaks of the nation Israel, He is speaking of a tribal nation, or more precise, a nation of 12 tribes. From the beginning, when to Jacob the 12 sons had been born (3a§12, Gen. 37:9-10).
And in the order of 12 tribes everything ends:
First, during the Greater Tribulation, 12,000 from twelve tribes come to faith (7abcd§67₁14).
Similarly, in the thousand-year kingdom of Israel, no longer is spoken of (merely) the Jewish people, the 2-tribe kingdom. God joins the stick of Judah and the stick of Joseph/Ephraim, the 10-tribe kingdom, into one stick, one nation (3b§12, Ezek. 37:15-28).

¤ However there is a problem. Of the twelve tribes, from which 144,000 are chosen, the original tribes of Dan and Ephraim are missing. Levi and Joseph have replaced them (Rev. 7:4-8).

Brother Branham said in the Seventh Seal Sermon that the reason had been idolatry in the midst of them (63-0324e, 7Seal Sermon, #190-228).

¤ At the beginning of the ten-tribe nation, no Danite or Efraimite had stopped the then king Jeroboam to build e.g. two places of idolatry among those two tribes (1Kings 12:25-13:30).

In our era of the Holy Spirit, it would never have been forgiven, but at that time was lived in the time of animal sacrifices, when the working of the Holy Spirit was not so strong (cf. e.g. John 14:26).

¤ It has been a temporary judgment of God based on the law given to the people of Israel, Deu. 29:16-21, <For you yourselves …. 18. Make sure there is no man or woman, clan or tribe among you today whose heart turns away from the LORD our God to go and worship the gods of those nations. …. 20. The LORD will never be willing to forgive him. Instead, His anger and jealousy will burn against that man, and every curse written in this book will fall upon him. The LORD will blot out his name from under heaven …. 21. ….>

But during the Greater tribulation time, both the nation of Israel and the sleeping virgins will be cleansed. After that, in the Thousand Year Sabbath Kingdom, the names of Dan and Ephraim are found {Ezek. 48 (11a§19-22)}.

¤

¤ In the millennial kingdom God accepts again the people and kingdom of Israel to represent Him until the end of the present heaven and earth (Acts 1:6-7).

After that, all mankind will be resurrected and judged according to their deeds, and the New Heaven and the New Earth with the New Jerusalem will appear (Rev. 20:1-21:2).

¤ The New Jerusalem will come down as a beautiful pyramid with a length, breadth and height of twelve thousand furlongs, about 1500 miles. Its wall is 144 cubits, about 252 feet heigh. With twelve gates named according to the twelve tribes of Israel. And with twelve wall foundations named according to the twelve apostles of the Lamb {2a§45, Rev. 21:12-14(-17)}.

It is the Mother of all believers born from above (1c§1-3 / 3a§12, Gal. 4:26).

¤ In His time, Jesus Christ chose twelve apostles, of which Judas Iscariot fell away (Lk. 6:12-16).

Next, the other apostles had tried to choose a substitute (Acts 1:15-26).

Though later, God chose His own apostle for the Gentiles, Paul {Rm. 11:13; Gal. 1:1 (5a§6(8)10)}.

¤ At the end, when everything is submitted to the Son, the Lamb, He will also submit to God (1Cor. 15:28).

Then, in the New Jerusalem (the Bride of the Lamb), God will dwell with His beloved ones (Rev. 21:1–22:5).

~ ~ ~

C12 (Revelation §1-22, Summary)

12a§1-22

Two thousand Years of Revivals

Shalom,
^ At the end follows my summary of the two-thousand-year era of the Christian churches, what God predicted already two thousand years ago according to His Ways (cf. 5a§6(8)10/9j§89₁156, Eccl. 3:14-15).
Prayer of them who are preparing to meet their Groom (Rev. 19:7-9),
Bert Hovestadt, (Street:) Pursimiehenkatu 4A19, (Town:) 15140 Lahti, (Country:) Finland
(Phone:) +358442808142 – (Email:) gijsberthovestadt@gmail.com

¤ By reading, hearing, and obeying what is written in the Book Revelation, you can become blessed (1a§1-3, Rev. 1:3).
The key word is revival. Living in continuous revival has been God's life instruction for believers, according to God's plan for seven church ages (1b§1-3).
¤ But during the revival of our last Laodicean church age there is no reason to be proud. Fortunately, in the mental pit of this revival God's glorious emergency plan can be noticed. Everyone is invited to meet the Lord Jesus Christ personally here on earth. It is an incredible promise (1c§1-3, Rev. 3:20).
How is it possible? God's prophet was needed for that. His coming was promised to us believers at the end of the church ages (cf. 1d§1-3).
¤
¤ In the circles of active believers, it has generally been taught that the middle part of the Book Revelation, the chapters 4-18, deals with the events of the Greater Tribulation time, which only then will be understood. Why? Why they would not open to the true believers. Why the biggest part of this Book opens only to those ones who have not prepared themselves to be ready for the Rapture?
Also it has been taught that the ten kings of whom Revelation speaks, would be the EU. But no more deeply studying in the Bible is needed to see that they represent the raw reality of present Communism and dictatorship (cf. 9k; 9l§89₁156 and 10a§18, Rev. 17:16).
¤ At the end there are two different churches. Believers who live according to God's predicted plans. And believers who do not live in harmony with God's entire Word, even though they could have a great anointing (5a and 5b§6(8)10).

It should be accepted, that to a prophet had been promised an understanding of the secrets of the seals and of everything. He would meet the Lord Jesus Christ as John the Baptist in his time {5c§6(8)10; 5d§6(8)10 (John 1:33-34)}.

¤

¤ The understanding of the secrets of the trumpets in heaven would belong to the Jewish people (8a§89₁156).

The judgments of the trumpets have already partially prepared the Israelites and the Jews to be in the right place, in Israel, where they will meet their (and our) Messiah (8b§89₁156).

¤ Though, the premature revelation of the secrets of the trumpets would wake up us believers. At that day 060621 I wrote that it meant, that the moment of the Rapture has come extremely near (cf. 8c§89₁156).

It would be the last moment to prepare to leave from here, all that remains on earth is sorrow (Rev. 19).

¤

¤ Already for ten years I have had to talk about the last year of Jesus' Coming on the clouds (1c§1-3).

Still more excited I was when 070821 the contents of the SEVENTH SEAL had come out impressively. Jesus Christ had appeared in a very concrete way (6m§6(8)10)!

¤ Finding Him is the core challenge of the end time of the church ages. It would set every believer on the move and in fire. There He is. There would have happened something.

The coming Rapture, when there would be the Presence of the Lord Jesus in the air, would take place on Easter 2022. In December 2021, I had felt forced by the Holy Spirit to announce this to many ones (see 12b§1-22).

¤ The Jewish and the Christian Easter was at the same time (seven days, 15/16.4 – 22/23.4.2022, and Friday 15.4 – Sunday 17.4.2022).

Four thousand years ago, Abraham had to offer his firstborn son, Isaac, as a burnt offering on Mount Moriah. Then God had intervened at the last moment (Gen. 22:2-11).

¤ Two thousand years later, Jesus Christ was crucified at Easter on the same place.

Did the Secret Coming of the Lord Jesus happen this year at Easter? On the other hand, in the same week, the Finnish version of this explanation had become visible in its entirety and without restrictions on the Internet. That might be the possible explanation in my case. It was God's intervening at the last moment (see also 12c§1-22).

¤

¤ The end-time church would have its own revivals when both the wheat and the weeds ripen (5b§6(8)10 and 8e§89₁156, Mat. 13:37-43).

So, there would be two different revivals at the same time. True prophets and anointed ones, and false prophets and anointed ones are experimenting their own REVIVING. Choose the right group {Mat. 24:24 (5a,5b§6(8)10)}!

Finland, End-Time Awakening

Shalom,
^ We would be living in the last moments of the church ages.
In the end, some of us are taken and others left. Some believers were ready, others not (Mat. 24:40-44).
Prayer of them who strive to be like-minded (Phili. 2:1-2), and strive to be, James 1:21-22: <Therefore, get rid of all moral filth and every expression of evil, and humbly accept the word planted in you, which can save your souls. 22. Be doers of the word, and not hearers only. Otherwise, you are deceiving yourselves.>

¤ For ten years I have been a member of the Kääntöpiiri church in the town of Lahti, Finland, and have been involved in its activities. I testified on 2021-12-15 at a prayer meeting, where all pastors were present and a total of about 15 people: I feel that the Holy Spirit has confirmed to me that Easter would be the Rapture of believers, of whom I hope to be one.
Too, I have testified of the same thing before, though not with a specified date (1c§1-3).
¤
¤ 2022-01-01 God's Spirit led me to watch the New Year's celebration in the town of Loimaa on Tv7, a Christian television station, all in Finland. There had been announced that our reverend Miko Puustelli would be the speaker for that evening.
But Miko's arrival was prevented because his family had been exposed to the Covid-19 virus at Christmas.
¤ It was a very wonderful spiritual meeting. I believe that the Holy Spirit Itself was speaking through the pastor and his wife, Teemu and Minna Tapio.
Here is my summary of what was said there:
¤ In God's spiritual army, every believer has his own task. And the seamless cooperation of believers would give the best result. It is A TIME OF BREAKTHROUGH when the Lord calls each of us. The departure command was needed so that we and many others surrender to acts of repentance and purification.
God has declared war against all forces of darkness here in Finland. Every involvement and cleansing should happen now, so that you are ready. Soon the Lord Jesus comes to get His Bride Church. After that, the Antichrist will take over the entire earth.
¤
¤ I saw a similar prophetic message on the same New Year's Day through the couple Jan and Joyce Cedercreutze at the same television station. Under the title Bread that satisfies hunger, water that quenches thirst.
And my summary of Joyce's words:

¤ There is a huge number of starving people who are crying out for food. A great cry rises to God. On different sides of the world. Help! Help! Help, Lord!

But God has heard it and ALREADY ANSWERED. Unfortunately, His answer has not been heard when, amid darkness, God did send the glad tidings of the Gospel.

¤ Through TV-7, the revival would have begun. Next, the waiting for the revival begins again. Each time is returned to the starting place. Not big enough numbers of people would have come to faith yet. However, it must be taken into account that the apostasy from Christianity has begun and that it affects the numbers that come to the faith. The revival around God's end-time prophet just hadn't been and hasn't been noticed. Same as in the past around God's prophet John the Baptist (1d§1-3, 2The. 2:3ba-4aa and Mat. 17:10b).

So we live very close to the Presence of our Lord Jesus in the clouds. One generation has already passed since the founding of the State of Israel. Every day the Rapture can be (3b and 3e§12, Lk. 21:32)!

¤

¤ The last revival of the church would be as special as the first (Acts 2:17-22).

Because, that is what the early apostles had referred to (Joel 2:28-32).

¤ Specifically, it was the revival before the Day of the Lord (Joel 2:31b).

Of the same day the prophet Malachi had spoken. God had promised to send the prophet Elijah to prepare the Messianic and Christian believers of the end-time before that day {6k§6(8)10, Mal. 4:(1-)6}.

¤ In addition to that, Joel's prophecy had spoken about autumn and spring rains, the first and last rains. (Compare these rains with Israel's rainless summer, Joel 2:23.)

First there had been the teachings of the first autumn rains, the perfect teachings of the Lord Jesus and of His apostles under the leading of the Holy Spirit. And after that, the revivals of the spring rains.

¤ The end-time must contain similar perfect teachings. Somehow these teachings should be rediscovered. Thus, this prophet and the messenger of the seventh church age have been one and the same person (5c§6(8)10, 8a§89$_1$156, Rev. 10:7).

After that, the revivals of the spring rains had started, until today. Personal revivals around the world with fasting, weeping and mourning for Judah and Jerusalem (Joel 2:12-3:1).

"THE LAST AWAKENING"

Shalom,
Thanks to all who endured in reading everything, Bert

¤ In the Book Revelation and in my consideration, I think revival has been its core word. And in the same way, the Holy Spirit has led me to write these last summary pages.

In a revival, faith is born. The Holy Spirit would be involved. There would be miracles and signs.

¤ When the last pieces and parts of the puzzle of the Book Revelation are put in the right place, it would be visible whether the puzzle is complete, or not? And so on. Are all the pieces used, or not? Or are the pieces just randomly put together?

God's puzzles are not two-dimensional. They are complicated. Inside of it would even be Life, as that is typical for God's Word (e.g. Acts 7:38).

¤ The edge pieces, the frame of the puzzle, or better said the puzzle's skin, would be this bouquet C12. The pieces on the outside would speak of a ready metamorphosis. Once my explanation has gotten a clear healthy shape, it would be PART OF THE REVIVING IN FINLAND. There the call for THE BREAKING THROUGH has been proclaimed (12b§1-22).

The Bible speaks of THE LAST REVIVING, e.g. with the parable of the ten virgins, which would happen all over the world at about the same time. Where believers await the Coming of the Groom (12a§1-22, Mat. 25:1-13).

¤ Virgins represent beautiful, pure, blameless believers. But when they are waking up, only very little time is left. Some have enough oil with them and some don't. In addition each of them stands alone.

What is most important? Light of the Oil of the Holy Spirit is needed, for example, to make the right decisions. Everyone needs Power of the Holy Ghost to hear from God the answers. Other ones' answers do not help. It is necessary to be one with God's Word. In the end-time of the churches it should be known who would be / have been God's Elijah-prophet. It is an eternal-life-important question! This is how God preordained the stage (1d§1-3, Mal. 4:1-6).

¤

¤ Seals, Trumpets, Woes and Bowls are what they are. Understanding everything in a right way is challenging. But there isn't much time left.

And the situation has not been easier for me. I have had to write about the date of the Presence of the Lord Jesus / Rapture and about all kinds of things against held beliefs. Thus everyone's faith is tested, and, God is looking for people who in the end-time have faith (cf. Lk. 18:8).

¤ Everyone has to leave their safe environment and look for the Lord Jesus somewhere else (1c§1-3, Rev. 3:20).

On the other hand, an ordinary passer-by could understand the events in the end-time described with help of the predictions of the book Revelation. It tells how the world looks like now, and what is about to start happening (0c§Preface, RECOGNIZE ....).
¤

¤ The rapture is the only Hope when fear and anxiety increase {Lk. 21:25(-33), 7a§67₁14}.

The times of the Gentiles have been fulfilled, since at least 1967 (Lk. 21:24, 3e§12).

¤ God's Word is both the beginning and the end of everything. Jesus had been with God, and had been God's Word from the beginning (John 1:1-2).

All things have been created through Him and for Him (John 1:3; Col. 1:16).

¤ Here He is our Life and our Light (John 1:4).

And we must become a part of Him, God's Word, God's Gospel, in order to enjoy this Light and Life (Col. 1:13-23).

¤ With God's Word everything will end. It will never pass away (Mat. 24:35).

In the same way my writing of God's Word had to become part of this Word and receive God's Confirmation.
¤

¤ Writing about the Book Revelation was challenging. Nothing may be added or taken away (cf. Rev. 22:18-19).

I started it with a group of believers. And gradually more groups have come. In that way it could be blessed according to the same Book (Rev. 1:3).

¤ Last year in December (2021) I had felt forced to say, that the Rapture would happen at Easter this year (2022). I had to announce that date to many and in many places (cf. 12b§1-22, Kääntöpiiri).

In that time I had no idea, that that date could be connected to the Finnish version of this explanation. However, at Easter all pages had become readable for free all over the world via the Internet.

¤ And the same thing happened with the English version. Too about a second date, 2022-08-07, I had had to write, when the page on the explanation of the Seventh Seal had come out in a very significant way (6m§6(8)10, 2021-08-07).

Instead of the Rapture event, the English version just before that date had become a good readable and widely available text. And the final confirmation and final seal was given by God on 2022.12.13 when I found the last main title (0§Copyright).

~ ~ ~ ~ ~ ~

Used Bible Verses / §-Page (13a)

1. Copy/Open link: https://ilmestyskirja-branham.com/book-revelation/

2. Click: "Three stripes button"

3. Click under 13ab: Bible Verses (_date)

4. Click: * Verses / §-page (13a)

Used Bible Verses, sorted (13b)

1. Copy/Open link: https://ilmestyskirja-branham.com/book-revelation/

2. Click: "Three stripes button"

3. Click under 13ab: Bible Verses (_date)

4. Click: * All verses, sorted (13b)

Used TaNaKh / Bible Books

T: Genesis = Gen.

T: Exodus = Ex.

T: Leviticus = Lev.

T: Numbers = Numb.

T: Deuteronomy = Deu.
- - - - - - - -
N: Joshua = Jos.

N: Judges
- - - -
K: Ruth
- - - - - -
N: 1 Samuel
N: 2 Samuel

N: 1 Kings = 1Ki.
N: 2 Kings = 2Ki.
- - - - - - - -
K: 1 Chronicles
K: 2 Chronicles

K: Ezra = Ezra

K: Nehemiah = Neh.
- -
K: Esther
- -
K: Job = Job

K: Psalms = Ps.

K: Proverbs = Prov.
- -
K: Ecclesiastes = Eccl.

K: Song of Songs/Solomon
- - - - - - - -

N: Isaiah = Isa.

N: Jeremiah = Jer.
- - - -
K: Lamentations
- - - - - -
N: Ezekiel = Ezek.
- - - - - -
K: Daniel = Dan.
- - - - - -
N: Hosea = Hos.

N: Joel = Joel

N: Amos = Amos

N: Obadiah

N: Jonah = Jonah

N: Micah = Micah

N: Nahum

N: Habakkuk = Hab.

N: Zephaniah

N: Haggai

N: Zechariah = Zec.

N: Malachi = Mal.
- - - - - - - - - - - - - - - -
Matthew = Mat.

Mark = Mrk.

Luke = Lk.

John = John

- -
Acts = Acts
- - - -
Romans = Rm.

1 Corinthians = 1Cor.
2 Corinthians = 2Cor.

Galatians = Gal.

Ephesians = Eph.

Philippians = Phili.

Colossians = Col.

1 Thessalonians = 1The.
2 Thessalonians = 2The.

1 Timothy = 1Tim.
2 Timothy

Titus = Titus

Philemon
- -
Hebrews = Heb.
- - - -
James = James
- -
1 Peter = 1Pet.
2 Peter = 2Pet.
- -
1 John = 1John
2 John
3 John = 3John
- -
Jude = Jude
- - - -
Revelation = Rev.

~ ~ ~

Personal notes

....

....

....

....

....

....

....

....

....

....

....

....

....

....

....

....

....

....